BLACK

AND

CATHOLIC

IN THE

JIM CROW

SOUTH

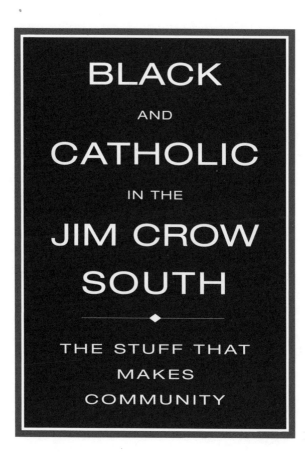

BLACK

AND

CATHOLIC

IN THE

JIM CROW

SOUTH

◆

THE STUFF THAT
MAKES
COMMUNITY

DANNY DUNCAN COLLUM

Paulist Press
New York/Mahwah, N.J.

Front cover images: "Chorister" courtesy Corbis Images. Used with permission. Holy Family Church and neighborhood images courtesy Susan Stevenot Sullivan. Used with permission.

Cover design by Trudi Gershenov

Book design by Sharyn Banks

Library of Congress Cataloging-in-Publication Data

Collum, Danny Duncan.
    Black and Catholic in the Jim Crow South : the stuff that makes community / Danny Duncan Collum.
        p. cm.
    Includes bibliographical references and index.
    ISBN 0-8091-4371-2 (alk. paper)
1. Holy Family Catholic Church (Natchez, Miss.)—Interviews. 2. Holy Family Catholic Church (Natchez, Miss.)—History. 3. Natchez, (Miss.)—Church history—20th century. 4. African Americans—Religion.
5. Southern States—Church history—20th century. 6. Catholic Church—Southern States—History—20th century. I. Title.
    BX4603.N34C65 2006
    282'.7622608996073—dc22
                                                    2005025495

Published by Paulist Press
997 Macarthur Boulevard,
Mahwah, New Jersey 07430

www.paulistpress.com

Printed and bound in the
United States of America

Contents

To Tim Murphy,
a true priest

Acknowledgments

This book began as a project of the Glenmary Research Center, which is affiliated with the Glenmary Home Missioners, a Catholic society of priests, brothers, and lay co-workers dedicated to mission in the rural South. The research center supports that mission by conducting research on Southern culture and religion, and especially on Catholicism in the South. As part of that work, back in the late 1980s, the Glenmary Research Center began working to document the history of Holy Family Catholic Church in Natchez, the first African American Catholic parish in Mississippi, and one of the oldest ones in the United States. The Glenmary Research Center has generously supported my work on this book. My thanks go out especially to Ken Sanchagrin, the center director, whose patience and faith were unwavering during the four years it took to bring this book to publication.

Although my name is on the cover, Tim Murphy and Susan Stevenot Sullivan did much of the work that made this book possible. In 1994, Reverend Tim Murphy, a Glenmary priest who had received training in collecting oral histories, conducted interviews with more than forty members, associates, and friends of Holy Family Church in Natchez. Those interviews were transcribed. Susan Stevenot Sullivan, working for the research center, then did the painstaking work of comparing the transcripts to the tapes and correcting them. She produced the final corrected copy of the transcripts from which I worked in composing this book. A full list of those interviewed for the project is included in the source notes at the end of this book. Reverend Peter Hogan, SSJ, historian of the Josephite order of priests, also made available interview transcripts, news clippings, and other documents from the Josephite archives in Baltimore.

My wife, Polly Duncan Collum, and our children, Christopher, Magdalena, and Joseph, were my constant companions throughout the work on this book. They gave me a powerful reason to continue when I sometimes felt like giving up.

Finally, thanks to the people of Holy Family Church in Natchez, who opened their homes and lives to strangers so that an important story could be told. This book is their offering to Mississippi and to the Catholic Church. I am also grateful to the people of St. Matthew's Church in Ripley, Mississippi, and St. Joseph's in Holly Springs—my home parishes during the work on this book. These two multiracial parishes provided me with a spiritual home, and a living vision of the beloved community for which so many brave souls have struggled and died. Thanks also to the people of St. Francis Catholic Church, the African American mission in my hometown of Greenwood, Mississippi, whose witness set me on the road I walk today.

Introduction

Just over forty years ago Mississippi was burning. A series of racially motivated murders and brutal repression of the movement to register black voters had drawn the moral outrage of the nation. Northern student volunteers were streaming into the state, followed by the national news media. All through the summer of 1964, the nation focused on Mississippi as the black citizens of the state sought, once and for all, to redeem the promise of the Emancipation Proclamation.

Those who are old enough, or have studied their history, may remember from that summer images of the three civil rights workers slain in Neshoba County, Mississippi, or of Fannie Lou Hamer leading the Freedom Democrat delegation to the Democratic National Convention at Atlantic City. But few are likely to know that in Natchez (Mississippi's second oldest city) a Roman Catholic parish, and its white priest, stood at the center of the African American freedom movement. In Natchez, Holy Family Church served as the headquarters for the area chapter of the NAACP. Its pastor, Father William Morrissey, became the vice-president of that organization and a statewide candidate on the Freedom Democrat ballot.

Holy Family was founded in 1890, when segregation laws were being implemented across the South, to provide a place of worship for the former slaves and mulatto offspring of Catholic plantation owners. But by the 1960s it had leaped the boundaries of that mission and become a center for struggle and hope. Black Catholics were a double minority in Natchez, as in most of the South. They were black in a predominantly white church, and were usually served by white pastors. But they were also Catholic in an overwhelmingly Protestant African American community. As many of the voices in this volume will attest, black Catholics in Mississippi faced, in the black community, many of the same myths and prejudices about their faith that have dogged white Catholics in the South. Still, Holy Family Catholic Church became, in the words of one member, "a beacon to the whole community." That's the story this book tells, in the voices of the people who lived it.

At the dawn of the twentieth century, African American scholar, W.E.B. Dubois predicted that "the question of the color line" would be the question of the century. And it certainly was in Mississippi. But on that preeminent question of race, the Mississippi Catholic Church occupied an odd no-man's-land. It was, and is, a mostly white institution, but it has never been a "whites-only" church. In the nineteenth century, it accepted slavery and supported secession, but it also ministered faithfully to the slave population. African Americans were never shut out of Catholic churches in Mississippi, as they were in some other denominations. But they were seated separately and, where they were numerous, provided with separate churches.

In the 1960s, the Catholic Church in Mississippi did not help lead the crusade for civil rights, but, virtually alone among predominantly white local institutions, it did come to actively support desegregation. Many white Catholics were part of the "massive resistance" to desegregation. But the church hierarchy also stood behind those priests, religious, and Catholic lay leaders who took to the streets for change. Some of the more prominent of these activists will be met in this book: Reverend William Morrissey, SSJ, pastor of Holy Family Church in Natchez during most of the 1960s, Marge Baroni, a white, Catholic Natchez laywoman and civil rights activist, Mamie Mazique a member of Holy Family and secretary of the Adams County NAACP, and many others.

Throughout the Jim Crow era, from 1890 to 1970, the Catholic Church in Mississippi was trying to be a nonracial institution in a society where race was primary. The church conceded much (often too much) to the Jim Crow order, but it also, here and there, bore witness to the possibility of a different one. It often made peace with the status quo, but it sometimes was an agent of startling change.

That pattern is mirrored in the story of Holy Family Catholic Church of Natchez, Mississippi. Holy Family was founded in 1890 as a separate parish for African Americans, a move that was much debated at the time. In that same year, Mississippi wrote its state constitution codifying the Jim Crow system of segregation and black disenfranchisement. Holy Family was the first African American parish in Mississippi, and one of the earliest in the nation, and it set the pattern for Catholic ministry among African Americans throughout the state. Holy Family is located in the city that, for most of the state's history, was the center of Mississippi Catholicism. Seen in this light, the Holy Family story can help us understand the Mississippi church's relationship with its African American people and the church's impact on race relations in the state.

There are many reasons why the Catholic Church has taken a racial stance different from that of most Southern white Protestants. Most of those reasons have to do with differences in the church itself. Unlike the other Christians in the South, Catholics are accountable to outside authorities. The local bishop rules, but he is appointed by the pope, and only the pope can remove him. So the teachings and directives of the global church—whether on race, liturgy, or birth control—do trickle down to the local Catholic congregation. The teaching may be diluted along the way, or treated with some local flavoring, but it does reach the average Catholic in the pew.

So when Rome said that no Catholic in good standing could be prevented from attending *any* Catholic church, this order had to be enforced in Mississippi. And it was. In 1958, Bishop Richard Gerow heard reports of threats directed against black Catholics attending St. Anne's Church in Fayette, near Natchez. The bishop made a surprise visit to announce that keeping black people out of Catholic churches in his diocese was a mortal sin, and one that could only be absolved by the bishop himself. Translated, this meant your local priest could absolve you for a mass murder, but if you kept black people out of church, you had to answer to the bishop. And until you did, you were doomed to hell. This was a serious exercise of power at a time when the spiritual authority of the hierarchy was unquestioned by most believing Catholics, and it kept the white Catholic churches in Mississippi open to black worshippers.

In addition, Mississippi has always been a mission diocese, unable to support itself either in finances or personnel. The majority of Mississippi's priests and nuns have come from the Northern states or directly from Ireland. So the church's leadership has never shared the local white community's intense investment in Mississippi's peculiar institutions of slavery and

Jim Crow. These white Northern missioners lived and worked in the African American community in Mississippi just as they would have among impoverished Italians or Poles in the North, but in Mississippi such a presence constituted an important breech in the wall of segregation. Since the early 1900s Holy Family in Natchez has been staffed by the Josephites, an order of (mostly white) priests devoted exclusively to African American missions.

The Catholic Church in the South is also set apart from the region's mainstream religious culture by the fact that it attaches religious significance to acts of temporal charity and questions of social justice. For Catholics, the drama of faith and salvation is lived out as much in this world as the next. This notion is embedded in the sacramental nature of the church's worship (i.e., the real presence of Christ in real bread and wine) and in the insistence that faith must be accompanied by good works for salvation to take effect. Catholics might not like the church meddling in their social practices, and they might disagree with the social teaching of their pastor, bishop, or pope, but they could never claim, as other Christians in the South often did, that the church's vocation was limited to the fate of souls in the hereafter.

The conflicting claims of local culture and custom set against the principles of a universal church kept Mississippi Catholics in some tension with their surroundings throughout the nineteenth and twentieth centuries. We can add to all of the above the fact that predominantly Catholic ethnic groups—such as Italians and Lebanese—were sometimes considered "not quite white" in a racialist's hierarchy of skin tones, and were certainly viewed as "foreign" in the Southern context. Then, in its early twentieth-century revival, the Ku Klux Klan lumped Catholics in with blacks and Jews as enemies of "white Christian civilization." Meanwhile, the growth of African American Catholic missions and schools was creating a population of educated black Catholics who expected to look white people in the eye as equals, and saw no reason to accept second-class status.

All of these tensions in the church and the state boiled over in a great confluence in the 1960s, when both were swept by their own (often intertwined) social revolutions—Vatican II and the civil rights movement. The Vatican II reforms turned the Catholic Church out toward the world and strengthened the church's emphasis on action for social justice and human rights. The proclamations of Vatican II did not make white Mississippi Catholics forsake their segregationist leanings. In fact, the church's eventual support for integration created deep divisions throughout the state. But Vatican II did make the rest of the U.S. church less tolerant of conditions in the South. And Catholic priests, nuns and laypeople, inspired by Vatican II, joined the army of activists intent on changing the South. As we will see in the Holy Family story, some of those Northern missioners already working in Mississippi were also emboldened by Vatican II to stop accepting the local racial customs and practices.

Black Catholics, of course, responded to the civil rights movement from the experience of oppression they shared with all black people and from the Christian hope they shared with black Protestants. Black Catholics became leaders in the movement, and foot soldiers, and in Natchez and other places around the state, black Catholics brought with them the institutional resources of the church. During the movement years, Reverend William Morrissey, SSJ, became vice-president of the Adams County Chapter of the NAACP (the first white officer of the organization in Mississippi history) and Mamie Mazique, an African American lay leader, was chapter secretary. The Natchez office of the NAACP was housed in the Holy Family parish hall throughout the middle and late 1960s.

As you will hear in this book, the civil rights years were violent in Natchez. A local activist, NAACP treasurer Wharlest Jackson, and another black man, Ben Chester White, were murdered in crimes that remain unsolved to this day. A third, NAACP chapter president George Metcalfe, was maimed by a bomb attack and moved away from Natchez in fear for his life. One civil rights demonstration, in 1965, ended with several hundred participants being arrested and bused to the state penitentiary at Parchman, more than two hundred miles away. There they were held for several days in conditions that can only be described as cruel and inhuman.

Catholic schools in Mississippi were integrated by order of the bishop in 1966, and in the years that followed some historically black Catholic schools were closed. In Natchez, the historically black St. Francis High School, attached to Holy Family parish, was closed in 1969. The K-8 school continues as Holy Family School. This created its own traumas for black Catholics, both from the loss of their own cherished institutions and from the difficulties encountered in the predominantly white schools.

The stories and voices collected here give a firsthand account of those events from the viewpoint of people who lived them. The aim is to leave the reader with some sense of what it was like to be black and Catholic in the twentieth-century South, and a clearer picture of the testimony the Catholic Church offered during the age of Jim Crow.

Chapter 1

Prelude

Lillian Johnson Adams

My great-grandmother came to Natchez as a slave. Her name was Catherine Coffee. She was sold in North Carolina, she said, when she was somewhere between twelve and fifteen years old. She and her little brother, Matthew, were sold at a slave auction to a buyer from Natchez, Mississippi, so they were sent down the Mississippi River on a boat to Natchez. Occasionally, the boat stopped and let them go ashore to do whatever they had to do, so her little brother got off the boat, and he went where he had to go, and then he went to pick some berries. He went too far, and the boat left him. They came on to Natchez. Matthew later told her that he cried and he roamed around. He didn't know anybody, and he didn't know where to go, but he found this family of people, a white family, and they took him in as their slave, and that's where he grew up.

Then in 1865 the slaves were freed. Matthew knew he was being sent to Natchez on that boat, so when he was free, he came to Natchez, and found his sister Catherine and they were reunited. I don't know how he did 'cause she lived way out in a rural area, but he did find her. She was married to a carpenter named Alfred Reed. He was supposed to have been part Indian, and she and her husband had something like five children. That was my great-grandmother.

Elsie Jackson

I guess about a month after I was born I was baptized at Holy Family Church. My entire family was Catholic—my mother and my father, all my grandparents and my great-grandparents. My great-grandmother was Margaret Ridley and she was married to Willie Ridley.

I'm not too sure how they became Catholic, but I'm sure that they were. My grandmother, Marguerite Davis, went to Catholic school here for twelve years. They couldn't pay tuition for the school. They were poor people, so they had to work for the Sisters. They worked cleaning bathrooms, cleaning the school, cleaning the convent, work like that. It was a big house, the convent, and it used to have a big back porch. My grandmother said the Sisters used to feed them on the back porch.

My grandmother was Indian-looking, but she had dark skin. She had long, long hair, but she wasn't a white-looking black, so it was kind of hard for her. At one time, our church and school was completely lighter-skinned people. My grandmother said she didn't suffer, but she always said it would be different. There would always be that difference. This is the way it was. Like most of those children that were doing the cleaning work were the darker-skinned kids.

Even when I was in school, there were more lighter-skinned people than dark-skinned. So, you know, way back it was even lighter. The church was full of light-skinned people. My grandmother always told me this is why the church was built. She said that it was built for Mr. Charlie's children.

Willie Fleming

Once Father Gaudette had the Cathedral School basketball team come over to our school. This would have been 1943 or maybe '44. We were going to practice basketball together. The white boys didn't mind. They come on over. They were already there playing ball. They was out there playing on the schoolyard; we didn't have a gym yet. But somebody didn't like it. Somebody told the police there was white boys over there at our school, and the police come and made them leave. It wasn't the school kids. Maybe the school kids might have told their parents or something, and they might have been the ones who did it. I don't know who did it, but the police found out, come there and run them away, told them to leave.

Joe Frazier

You felt a safety net around you if you went to Holy Family Church or if you went to the Catholic school because there was always somebody there to come speak up for you. For instance, some people who may have gotten into trouble, Catholics or non-Catholics, if they didn't know anywhere else to go they would come and ask one of the priests. Can you get my child out of this? Or can you go and talk to the people down there? It just so happened at that time a lot of the people in power in Natchez were Catholics. They have prominent Protestants now, but back then St. Mary's Cathedral had the powers that be, so if some of our priests could go and talk to some of those people, it made a big difference. The community knew that, and we at Holy Family knew that, too.

I remember there was a big guy who went to our church, but he had his Saturday nights, and on one of them he was stopped by policemen, and I don't know whether he did something or what, but they hit him with clubs. They beat him, and they put him in jail and didn't let him get any medical attention. When, I think it was Father Mulroney, and maybe he had an assistant, Father Flanagan, well, when they heard about it, they went down, and they kind of turned the place out, and they got some lawyers, some of the people who were powers at the Cathedral to go down, and they went and got him out of jail and carried him to the Charity Hospital. I personally know of that case because I remember seeing the guy with big lacerations where the policemen had beat him with the clubs.

The priests and nuns were the only white people working in the black community back then. Personally, I know that I handled myself around white people in the community at a much more comfortable level because all my teachers and priests were white. I had dealt with them on a personal basis without fear. I was able to speak more freely. Our parents would say, "Watch what you say around the white people. Watch what you say." Well, those of us who went to the Catholic school, even though we knew what to say, we did not have to watch our every word. We felt more on a comfortable level.

It may have been surprising with some of them, the ease with which we'd talk. And we'd look people in the eye where many black people had been told don't look the white person in the eye. If he says something just look down and go on, 'cause he'll think you're an uppity nigger or something. Oh, I've been told that so many times, but I didn't feel it because I had looked the nuns in the eye. In fact, with Sister Norbert, you had to have eyeball contact. That's the first place I heard that. "Mister Frazier, eyeball contact. Look at me when you're talking to me." And you can't just turn that off and on like water. I think all of us dealt with our white brothers and sisters on a different level. We did not have that fear or that looking down.

Vernon Williams

I was baptized in 1938, when I was fourteen. I remember that well. I don't guess you'd ever forget that unless you were baptized in infancy. I had a job. I was working down on Franklin Street at a place called the Royal Garden. It was a beer garden. It was nothing but a saloon actually, but we called it a beer garden. The baptism was on Saturday, so I had to take off. I told them, "I got to go to get baptized." And I'll never forget. There were about four or five guys working with me there; everybody was giving a big laugh. "Hey, you going to get baptized?" I said, "Yeah, man, I'm going to get baptized and be a Catholic." Father Mulkeen baptized me that Saturday, and I left the baptism to come on back to work in the beer garden. Yeah, came on back to work that day and back to Mass that Sunday.

At that time people didn't take as much into the baptizing of a child as we do now. They didn't make too much of it whether you be a Catholic or a Baptist or what. Now, a Baptist would always have a great big Sunday for baptizing around here. Yeah, we'd go to them. I would go out there on the creek, down to the river, or wherever they held it. Oh, and they'd enjoy it because they'd do the old-fashioned thing. Give me that old-fashioned religion; good enough for me.

I've heard a lot of bad talk about the Catholics. They say, "Man, you go down there, and you got to confess to the priest and things like that." It don't matter. It wasn't embarrassing to me to hear that from them. A man would say, "I don't understand why you want a religion like that," but that's the way it was.

Of course, my family, all of them was just Baptist, Baptist, Baptist all the way down. Then a few of us got baptized Catholic, and that was through. They called Father Mulroney the Baptizer. He had so many converts. He had converts all over. I had a cousin; he was baptized, too. A lot of them he baptized hadn't been back since. I can't talk about them because I don't go too much myself now. But I guess Father Mulroney baptized more people in this area than anybody.

Reverend Shead Baldwin

During the 1960s, Holy Family Church, as a parish, took out a life membership in the Natchez NAACP, and so that made the whole parish involved in the movement. Holy Family was the only church in town that took out a life membership. Most of them were afraid. In later years, I think the Zion Chapel Church took out a life membership.

And our headquarters was at Holy Family. The NAACP office was housed at Holy Family from 1965 to 1970. This made some of the whites, especially, have kind of a bad attitude toward Holy Family Church. That's where all the action would take place. They kept breaking into our office because we kept our own records on the voter registration drive.

Every time we'd make a drive, we'd put the names of the people up, and they wanted to get our records to try to find out how many registered voters we had and all that.

Now the black community was always with Holy Family. They always helped us and, in fact, a lot of non-Catholic black kids go to Holy Family School. Anything that come up at Holy Family, it concerns us, too, you know, because the Klansmen hate the Catholics as bad as they hate us.

Louisa Quinn

I think it was toward the end of 1964. We went to a meeting on Saturday morning at Beulah Baptist Church, and the city police came and ordered us all to go home. When we wouldn't go home, they arrested us at the church and carried us to the City Auditorium and told us they were carrying us there to get us off the street. From the City Auditorium, they had buses, and they carried us to Parchman that Saturday night. I think we stayed Sunday and Monday, and we got out that Tuesday. But it was a horrible experience, I can tell you that.

When we got to Parchman and got off the bus, they give everybody medicine—a laxative, and then they locked us up about four to a cell. No mattress on the bed, no covers, just iron cells. One commode, no toilet paper. I'm telling you it was horrible.

Now the men, they stripped them naked and ran water hoses on them. It was the fall of the year. It wasn't really cold, but it wasn't warm either. I can remember it was fall because it was cotton-picking time. At Parchman they told us they was going to make us pick cotton, but they didn't.

About four buses of us went up there that Saturday night, I think, and they were full, so it was a hundred and something people, I guess. Then they brought some more women and men from Natchez later on that next day, and they come in there that Monday morning for a day. So it might have been something like three hundred arrested in Natchez in all those two or three days because they continued to bring them in there. We got out that Tuesday, and it was a lot of them still up there that they had brought in.

Sidney Gibson

I think that me being a Catholic played a big role in the way I've been active through my whole life, in the union at International Paper, and in the civil rights movement. My faith taught me compassion, understanding, and patience. That played a big role in how much you achieve, especially in leadership. I think I learned all of that. The nuns had a great deal to do with it. I always had an awful lot of respect for the nuns. I was always crazy about them. It was almost like they were a bunch of little angels or something; they seemed to have so much patience and care for the students, and I guess it just rubbed off. I think they had a lot to do with me and my general attitude about things. Their attitude of caring about other people goes a long way.

Also, in my time growing up, I think the Catholic religion here was the most liberal and tolerant of all the religions, period. I think there was more tolerance in the Catholic Church than in the Protestant churches, because black and white people were going to Catholic churches together here long after they quit going to church together as Protestants. Once they started building black Protestant churches, black people couldn't go to white churches at all. But from the very beginning, until now, black people still could go to

Cathedral. I think that made a lot of difference as far as the teaching of tolerance is concerned. I think it impacted my life greatly because I don't think the majority of the people in this community see me as a Catholic man; they see me as a compassionate person. That's where they accept me.

People ask me if I was afraid during the civil rights movement. It's the truth; you get scared, and a lot of times we marched at night. We were always near the front of the line, and we believed if someone was going to be shot with a high-powered rifle, it was going to be some of us. We knew this was a Klan stronghold and we had decided that even though we were afraid, it was something that was going to have to be done. I told my wife. She used to discuss it with me. I said, "Well, I've had a full life. I've done right things, and I'm proud of it. If this is the time it's going to happen, this is the time it's going to happen. Somebody's got to get out there and do it."

That's what you do. We was some scared people. And we didn't deny it among one another; we discussed it. That's what gave us the courage to keep going.

Ora Frazier

From way back, it just seemed that Holy Family kind of stood out, you know. People within the black community kind of looked up to Holy Family. I think it had a lot to do with the school. And a lot of people came to special services like the midnight Mass. I mean, the church would just be packed with people because the other churches didn't have that. Now, some of the others have come along with midnight services, but in those days Holy Family would just be packed with so many non-Catholics. I think they felt that Holy Family had something that they didn't have.

And a lot of them, non-Catholics, even now, talk about priests that were here and what they did, you know, in the community and how they used to get kids out of the little joints and pool halls, even though the children were not Catholics. You know, parents really appreciated that. So, even now, I think, we kind of serve as a beacon in this community. It's in that little booklet about the church. It says it's like dropping a rock on the water and the ripples spread. I think that's what has happened with Holy Family. The ripple has just sort of reached out and made an impact on the Natchez community.

Chapter 2

"Historic Natchez"

The place is the Natchez City Auditorium on a cool Wednesday night in early spring. The auditorium is a red brick building with a white domed roof that sits on a downtown street just a block from the river. The streets around the auditorium are full of people walking in from their hotels, or from distant parking places. A bus is stopped in the auditorium drive unloading a cargo of senior tourists from up North. As the people enter, they present their tickets and are handed a program printed on buff-colored paper. On the front of the program is a silhouette drawing of a lady sitting under a parasol. She is wearing a long dress with puff sleeves, and her petticoats and skirt are spread far and wide about her. She's being approached by a frock-coated gentleman who carries a bouquet and is raising his top hat to the lady. Below this illustration is written in italic script, "The Historic Natchez Pageant 2002."

Inside the auditorium, the hardwood floor is cleared and waxed to a shine. A stage rises at the far end, and rows of old wooden theater seats are banked up on all sides. The seats are about three-quarters full, not bad for midweek.

A few minutes after eight, the lights go out. A spotlight hits the stage to reveal a little white girl, floating on a cloud of ruffles and lace, holding a large placard that reads, "The American Flag Triumphant." She takes a seat at one side of

19

the stage. At a podium on the other end, stands a thickly built white man, of about sixty, with thinning hair and metal-rimmed glasses. He is wearing a blue frock coat with tails, a frilly white shirt, and a ribbon bow tie. He begins to read about the early history of Natchez in a deep voice that bears the gentle, rounded accent of the Southern planter class. As he speaks, another spot hits the floor at the back of the hall and tracks the entrance of a series of costumed figures representing the various eras of Natchez history. There is a white man done up as the elaborately feathered Indian, "Great Sun," chief of the sun-worshiping Natchez tribe. He is followed by frontiersmen in coonskin and fur, a French governor, some Englishmen, and a Spaniard, each carrying his national banner. Finally comes a group of blue-coats, complete with a drummer boy, presenting the flag of the United States of America. At the end of the tableaux, all of the figures are massed on the stage, under the stars and stripes, uniting the many strands of Natchez history and heritage. There has been no mention of Africa. The people on stage are all white.

Coming into Natchez on Highway 61, the landscape is riddled with metaphor. Start with the name of the road. It's the U.S. route that tracks the course of the Mississippi River from Minneapolis to New Orleans. Countless blues singers made it famous from one end while a young Bob Dylan immortalized it from the other. But on the outskirts of Natchez, Highway 61 could be any road to anywhere. To get to historic Natchez you'll follow the signs for "Business 61." It's also called D'Evereux Road, and it is lined with fast food joints, chain stores, and budget motels.

Then there is D'Evereux itself. It rises like a Greek temple from the left-hand side of the road, surrounded by several acres of rolling, manicured lawn and ancient live oaks dripping with moss. It is one of the biggest and most lavish of Natchez's legendary antebellum mansions. At the end of its circular driveway, the structure is festooned with white columns and circled at the top by a widow's walk that surrounds a cupola the size of some people's houses. At first sight, you might be struck with awe at the wealth and ambition the place represents. On second thought, you might contemplate the horrid concentration of blood, sweat, and stolen labor behind each brick and portico.

But you might be jolted out of your reverie by the sight of D'Evereux's next-door neighbor—another emblem of white power—the First Baptist Church of Natchez. A structure of similar size and surroundings, the church stands by D'Evereux. In fact it was carved from her side, on acreage purchased from the D'Evereux estate. There, at the edge of the city, the neighboring structures stand like a two-headed Cerberus guarding the gates of white Southern "heritage."

But don't linger on that image too long, either. Within seconds you'll arrive at the "Forks of the Road" where several major thoroughfares intersect. Today it is just a confusing tangle of asphalt and cement, with a small historical site marker misplaced in its center. But in the old days it was the sight of the second largest slave market in America. Human beings were sold almost everywhere in historic Natchez. You could set up a slave auction on any street corner, and many people did. But here at the Forks of the Road was the grand shopping mall of the trade in human souls. In the early days it was filled with newly arrived Africans just up from New Orleans. Later, with the trade from Africa banned by law, the shelves were stocked with men, women, and children from the upper South who had the misfortune to be sold down the river (yes, that's the origin of the phrase).

The rest of your trip into downtown Natchez will take you past the homes of the people who were once sold at the Forks of the Road. On the other side of the Forks, D'Everaux Road becomes St. Catherine Street. It takes you through some of the poorest quarters of black Natchez, but it is also dotted with a few restored homes of the black professional class dating back to the nineteenth century. On the left side of St. Catherine, about halfway between the Forks and downtown, is Holy Family Catholic Church and School.

Present-day Natchez has a population of about 22,000, but its downtown area has the feel of a much larger, and more urban, place. It doesn't seem like a Mississippi county seat. The streets are lined with dense rows of nineteenth-century commercial buildings, many hung with full-length wrought iron balconies on the second floor. Every other block seems to harbor a drinking establishment. They call out to you from sidewalk awnings—The Courtyard Lounge, The Pearl Street Cellar, Dimples', J.R.'s Corner Saloon, and so forth. This is noteworthy in an overwhelmingly Baptist state that was officially "dry" until 1966. In fact, downtown Natchez seems more like a misplaced slice of New Orleans.

Natchez was always different from the rest of Mississippi. It has more Catholics and fewer Baptists. The Spanish brought the Catholic Church to town, and Natchez was the seat of the Mississippi diocese into the 1960s. Catholics are a minority here, but an influential one. Natchez was also the only town in Mississippi that, like New Orleans, had a significant population of free black people, some of whom were prominent in business and even owned their own slaves.

Natchez is different from the rest of Mississippi because it has a history that is much older than the state of Mississippi. Named for a now-extinct Indian tribe, Natchez was an important trading center long before the arrival of Europeans. The Natchez Trace, now a national parkway, was once an Indian trade route that ran down to Natchez from what is now Nashville, passing from the territory of the Cherokee through that of the Creek, Chickasaw, and Choctaw. The present city of Natchez was established as a trading post by the French in 1705 and later in that century was controlled by Spain. It was an important river port for almost a century before it became an American possession. Some of that heritage is still visible almost two hundred years later.

As you get closer to the river, and closer to the heart of old Natchez, antebellum residences appear on the streets. These range from the relatively modest homes of merchants, to mansions with grounds and outbuildings that cover a full city block. These structures are not from the French or Spanish periods. Most date from the great explosion of cotton wealth that hit the Deep South in the 1840s and 1850s after the invention of the cotton gin.

The city rests on a bluff that rises sharply from the east bank of the river. At its edge, you can look out across a vast flood plain on the Louisiana side. Many of the planters who built mansions in Natchez owned land in Louisiana. They could stand on their upper-floor balconies and see their slaves toiling in the fields across the river. Below the bluff is Under-the-Hill, the seedy district next to the riverboat landing. In the city's glory days, Under-the-Hill was famous for drunkenness, gambling, violence, and prostitution. Today, it is home to a number of saloons and a riverboat casino.

The frill-layered girl reappears from side-stage with another placard: "Picnic at Concord" it says. The lights go up, and the floor of the auditorium is teeming with white people—several dozen of them. There are men and women, boys and girls of all ages, strolling, sitting under shade trees, frolicking, and playing games. All are decked in elegant nineteenth-century dress. At one end of the floor a group of boys are pitching horseshoes, while the narrator tells about one of the oldest Natchez family dynasties—the Minors— whose founder, Stephen, served as deputy governor under the Spanish in the late 1700s. When the narration is finished, taped fiddle music rolls from the speakers and the picnickers on the floor gather into several clusters and pair up for square dancing.

This is a picnic at the Minor place (dubbed Concord), circa 1840. The black people who would have prepared and served the picnic food are absent and unmentioned; so are the ones who would have played the dance music.

Natchez is very self-conscious about its image and its history. The city's economic survival depends in large part upon the income from "pilgrimage" months in March and October when dozens of the old mansions are opened for public tours. The pilgrimages began in 1932, at the depths of the Great Depression. They were begun, and are still sponsored by, the ladies' garden clubs of the city. Natchez tourism enjoyed a huge boost in the wake of *Gone with the Wind,* and the industry has grown consistently ever since. This economic dependence has only served to deepen an already existing devotion, among the city's upper crust, to a myth of the Southern past. The image portrayed in the pilgrimage is of a time when plantation owners were not greedy slave-driving exploiters, but philosopher-kings and patrons of the arts. They were a New World aristocracy, presiding over a kingdom of beauty, order, and civility, until it was all brought down by meddling Yankees.

Like any good myth, this one is sustained by a tiny germ of truth. There was a time when a number of white people in the Deep South grew fabulously wealthy and spent much of their wealth on a lifestyle of luxury and refinement. This truth cannot be denied. The physical evidence is there in the more than two dozen homes on the Natchez pilgrimage trail. But it is only a half-truth, and, as we all know, that can be worse than a lie. The other half of the story is, of course, that the planters' display of wealth and culture depended entirely upon the stolen labor of a kidnapped and captive people. And the refusal to acknowledge this equally self-evident fact poisons everything else about Southern history.

But the falsification involved in the Natchez myth is even more complicated than this straightforward evasion of moral responsibility would suggest. If you start with Jamestown, antebellum Southern history covers a period of some 250 years. In Natchez the antebellum era lasted 155 years. The world immortalized in the Natchez pilgrimage existed for one decade—the 1850s. It blew in like the wind, and then it was gone.

In March 2002, I visited Natchez with my family. We went on some pilgrimage home tours and attended the "historical" pageant staged four times a week during pilgrimage month. We were astounded at the denial and willful amnesia about the very existence of African Americans. Repeatedly the tour guides were asked, "What is that building behind the big house?" And the answer was always, "I think they rent that out." Or, "It's used for storage." If the questioner pressed,

"But what was it in the old days?" the guide pretended ignorance. The building was, of course, the residence of the house slaves, but the pilgrimage ladies' wall of denial was impenetrable.

Meanwhile the "Historic Natchez Pageant"—which carries the content and context for the pilgrimage event—has no black characters and made no reference to the existence of black people, enslaved or otherwise. The introduction referred to "Indians, Frenchmen, the British, and Spaniards..." all of whom "left their mark on this river city." The casual visitor to Natchez today would find considerable evidence of a British influence, and a few Spanish and French place names. The only Indians to be found are motel owners of the South Asian variety. But the African mark on the city, unacknowledged in this version of history, is plain, and perhaps even dominant.

If you know anything about Southern history, a walk through historic Natchez and its pilgrimage events can be downright eerie—like a *Twilight Zone* episode. The closest parallel I can think of in real life would be the old East German tours of the concentration camps that interpreted the Nazi genocide solely in terms of anti-communism and omitted all mention of the Jews.

It's 1861, and the glamour of war has intoxicated the upper crust of the Deep South. On the pageant floor, dozens of young men are costumed in the dress gray uniforms of Confederate army officers. They waltz gaily with the town's prettiest young girls who are done up in taffeta and lace dresses with enormous hoop skirts. This is a farewell ball for the brave young men who will soon march off to make quick work of the Yanks, or so they think. The scene is a frozen snapshot of the grand, deluded moment of romantic glory that fell between secession and the bloody reality of Virginia battlefields.

At the end of the dance, the floor empties and the room goes dark. The taped music plays "Dixie" and a lone young man leaps onto the floor carrying a giant Confederate flag. He screams like a banshee as he hops across the floor. Finally he leaps onto the stage and strikes a defiant pose. The spotlight settles on the Stars and Bars, and the hall goes dark again.

After a moment, the spotlight hits the back of the hall, and the drum corps from the opening tableaux returns with the Stars and Stripes. They march across the floor toward the stage, and the spotlight follows them. When they reach the stage, it is empty. The Confederate wildcat has slunk away, unremarked and unnoticed, through a side door. Four years of bloodshed and eleven years of Reconstruction miraculously evaporate, as the taped music shifts to "God Bless America." The narrator concludes his spiel, "...the South valiantly sought to become a part of a reunited nation, under God, with the American flag triumphant."

Still historic Natchez does change, though usually under forcible coercion. It took a long, bloody war, but there are no more slave markets in Natchez, and there are no more slaves. The system of legal segregation that prevailed from 1890 to the 1960s fell before the combined efforts of the African American community, a few white allies, and the federal courts. In fact, the very City Auditorium, where the "Historic Natchez Pageant" is performed, served as a holding pen after mass arrests of civil rights demonstrators during those battles.

And change comes even to the hallucinatory world of the pilgrimage industry. The 2002 pilgrimage pageant was, after all, the first to be billed as "The Historic Natchez Pageant." For decades before it was known, accurately enough, as "The Confederate Pageant." This change came after the year in which Mississippi underwent a wrenching controversy about the use of the Confederate emblem on the state flag. A gubernatorial commission proposed a new flag design. The legislature passed the buck and called a referendum, which received international publicity. In the end, Mississippi voters decided by a large majority to keep the Stars and Bars. After the vote, there was talk of an economic boycott against the state. The NAACP had recently waged a boycott against South Carolina, where the Confederate flag flew from the roof of the state capitol. The boycott did serious damage to the economy of Charleston, which, like Natchez, depends heavily on visitors to its antebellum mansions and historic sites. So the title of the pageant was changed, though, I'm told, the content was the same as in preceding years.

This wasn't the first change in the pageant. Black people were not always absent from the production. In times past some of them played the parts of plantation slaves in scenes that included a cotton-field tableau of the harvest season. This ended when the garden clubs could no longer find any black people willing to take the slave roles. The 2002 pageant did feature one black participant. She was a young girl who appeared in a ballet segment put on by a local dance academy. I later learned that, a few years earlier, her older sister had been a student at the same academy and had been refused the chance to perform in the pageant. In 2002, the dance teacher insisted that the garden clubs let her bring all her students, or forget about the ballet.

This is the context for the story that follows. The African American families, who founded Holy Family

Church, and all of those who have kept it alive over the decades are an inextricable part of the city of Natchez and its history. They dug the foundations, laid the brick, cooked the food, tended the children, cared for the sick, and buried the dead. Many of them also took leading roles in the struggle to transform the city, and they helped write the first chapters of its post–Jim Crow history.

Chapter 3

Early Days

Lillian Johnson Adams and Laura Hoggatt *(sisters)*

Adams: So my great-grandmother, Catherine Coffee, who was a slave in North Carolina and in Natchez, married a man named Alfred Reed. And he was a very skilled carpenter. He helped to build Mistletoe out on Pine Ridge and some of the other antebellum homes out in the countryside.

Hoggatt: But he was not a slave. He was what they called a free person of color.

Adams: I think he was free, you know. They didn't talk like he was a slave, but my great-grandmother, Catherine Coffee, was a slave, and he married her. They had about five children, too. Now Catherine Coffee seemed to have been part Indian. My mother always referred to us as being Indian also. But my other great-grandfather was white.

Hoggatt: I saw one picture of him. He had long hair and a long beard. So my grandmother, Jane Dunbar, was mulatto. She was. Don't ask me about them, because her father's family, they were white people, and, at that time, they didn't recognize the children they had by blacks. And they were these high-society whites, you know, so you didn't dare say that you were a member of their family, so we don't know nothing about them.

Our grandmother, Sarah Reed Johnson, told us all about this. In fact, my great-grandmother told me about the trip from North Carolina, about being sold and all that. And this is her daughter, which is my grandmother. They told us all about it.

We come up in a big family; there was twelve of us. We were real devoted to our grandparents on that side, and we used to love going to see them, and they would always tell us things about how they lived as slaves and what freedom they had and what freedom they didn't have, and how they met each other, and things like that. Like, my mother's grandmother said that she was owned by a family over in Natchez, and somewhere they had a barbed-wire fence with guards that walked those lines to keep the slaves from running away. And the people that she worked for would let her off at night to go home and visit her family. So this man was a guard, a trusted black, and that's where she met him, going back and forth to her family at night. And, when she was free, they got married. That was Grandma Jane, and her husband was Collins Dunbar.

Adams: They never talked about actually being mistreated as slaves. There are some things you've seen where slaves were beaten, but my grandmother never told us anything about that. But she said that her masters—that's what she called them—were real strict. You had to do whatever you were told to do. This was a way of life. If you were supposed to survive, you would have to obey your master. That was it.

Charles Posey

My great-grandmother was Sally Ann Mills. She was part Indian. She never told me that, but I could see the characteristics there. She was a steady old lady. I remember the time she used to call my grandmother. She had a loud voice. She would call at the gate and bring food. She'd pack it on her head. I think I was about six or seven years old, but that's something I can remember. She was a remarkable old lady, my great-grandmother. She was a maid, so to speak, and she worked for a prominent white family, the Hunters. She lived to be something close to a hundred years old.

Sally Ann Mills had been a slave. Her mother was named Harriet Stovall, and the land that we own out Providence Road was deeded to her. I can't think of the name of the white person that deeded her the land. It could've been Stovall. And Providence Plantation is right next to the land that we own now, so evidently she was a slave at this particular place, and she was freed. From her, there was Sally Ann and Susan, my grandmother, and my mother from there on.

Willie Fleming

My mother and father and family all grew up around here, out in the country around Cranfield—right here on this road. My father was born down there in that old house where we was raised up. I knew my grandfather and grandmother on my father's side, but I only knew my grandfather on my mother's side. That grandfather was born here, but either his father or his grandfather—I'm not sure which—came from England. He was white, but he had a black wife. He came here with his brother, and his brother did the same—had a black wife. That was the Flemings.

My mother's people all come from a place out here they call Freewoods. They call it that because it's mostly Indian and mixed race. So my mother's people were part Indian. White people started going back in there around Freewoods staying with those Indians, and that's how they come about. I don't know when the blacks got mixed up in there. It would have been later in the years because most of them didn't have no black blood in them at all. It was Indian and white, and they wasn't classified as white or Indian. I don't know what they classified them as. I get all my information about this from my cousins, the ones that used to live out there. They know all about it. They showed me around the old Indian mounds and stuff, all still out there. They live out there now; they don't look nothing like Indians anymore. They were mixed up, I guess, with Indians and whites.

They called it Freewoods because they never had slavery in there. That was in Franklin County, right out the end of Liberty Road. You go out the end of Liberty Road and go down Highway 33 about a mile or so to Knoxville, Mississippi. It's right back in the woods behind Knoxville. There'd be a wood-yard out there. It's way back in the woods. Back in those days, the only thing that could go in there was a horse or a wagon—mule wagon, ox wagon, or something like that. It was way back in, four or five miles back, nothing but woods. If it rained, you couldn't come out of there. You had to stay back in there until the water went down. And, by them being half Indian, Indian and white mixed up with something, there never was no slavery or nothing back in there. They just lived back there independently. Nobody ever fooled with them.

Vernon Williams

My great-grandfather, Austin Williams, was a Civil War soldier. I don't know what side he fought for, the Confederacy or the Union, but I do know he was a veteran.

Different stories get handed down about that. His children, and my aunts, and all, would call him Papa, instead of Daddy or something like that. It was Papa Austin and Ma Adaline. She was his wife, and he bought her out of slavery. Now, a lot of that history I got from hearsay, but that's what I understand happened, that he bought her.

I saw a picture of Papa Austin. He was with a congregation on the porch of Beulah Baptist Church. He wore a big mustache. At that time, it was white, and his hair was white, too. He was light-skinned. And Ma Adaline was dark, very dark. She was tall and thin, very thin and close to six feet tall—and very, very stern. When she said, "Come," you come.

When I was a little bitty boy, I stayed with her, along with my brother and two or three of my cousins. And when she said, "Now, you come in, and you going to eat at six o'clock," you'd eat at six o'clock. If you didn't, too bad. You didn't get yours because she said that's what time you do it. She was just a strong, stern woman. I never will forget her. She was what you call the matriarch of the family. Papa Austin would have been dead then for a long time.

She was also a doctor. You ever seen Granny on *Beverly Hillbillies?* She was that type of doctor. She believed she was, too. She'd mix up some kind of herbs and things for any ailment you had, and she would get it done, too. I don't know of anybody she killed, but she'd cure sore throat, fever, a bellyache, or anything like that. Anybody could call her; they called her Aunt Adaline, and she'd come over and see about 'em. If they was having babies, she'd go there and midwife in the home. She had all kinds of stuff in the cabinet. I remember seeing her mixing all this stuff together. I don't suppose it was a voodoo potion; I don't think that, although it might've been.

A kid would get so sick; now we might call it strep throat, but back then we'd say their palate was down. And she would mix some stuff up—some spices—on a little spatula, like a tongue depressor, and reach down in there and lift the palate, and they wouldn't be so sick. I stepped on a nail once, a rusty nail, and it went through my foot, came out the top, the nail did. You wouldn't think of not going to the doctor, now. But she bathed it in coal oil—kerosene, we'd call it now—put some fat meat on the bottom and tied it around with a rag. I walked on the heel wearing that for about three or four days, I guess. I guess I was lucky, because I should have had lockjaw or something, but I didn't. And that's the only medicine they had on it, that salt meat and kerosene.

I don't remember her telling anything about slavery days. She did say one thing that I remember because we all couldn't understand it. She said she was a girl out in the fields up there, and she could hear the cannons roaring up in Vicksburg, or Port Gibson, up in that area. She remembered hearing them cannons roaring because the last of the cannons roared in 1865.

Selma Mackel Washington

Now Robert H. Wood had a daughter who was Stella Wood Dent. And she had a daughter who was Selma Dent Mackel, and, then, I am Selma Mackel Washington, and we've carried the name Selma from Wood's other daughter. Her name was Selma Wood Dinelli. She died early in life, and didn't have any children, so my grandmother was the only one that carried the family on.

So Robert H. Wood had two children—both daughters. And one of them, Stella Wood Dent, was my grandmother.

She didn't tell me much about him. Sometimes she and my mother might be sitting on the porch or in the kitchen, and she would say, "Selma, do you remember when Papa did thus-and-so?" And I would hear them refer to the time that he was sheriff and they lived in the jail or some facility somewhere. But, unfortunately, I didn't get much of it.

Robert Wood had both of his daughters baptized Catholic at St. Mary's. I don't know how Robert Wood became a Catholic. I do remember seeing something that had been written about a time that the town had allotted $200 to the Catholic asylum, and they wanted to rescind the donation, but then Robert Wood stuck up for the donation. But that's basically all I remember about him being Catholic.

As far as what I knew of him as my great-grandfather, apparently, he was well-devoted to his family. He seemed to spend a lot of time with them. I don't really know too much about him otherwise. I know that he had operated a store in the Washington area just out from Natchez; that was after he had done all his political work. He had been very much interested in politics. He and John R. Lynch [Reconstruction-era congressman, also from Natchez] had been friends together, and he did quite a lot of the public work. He was interested in helping the public.

As far as I know, Robert Wood was never a slave. His mother was Susie Harris, an African American woman, and his father was a white doctor—Dr. Robert Wood. Now, I don't know if there was a marriage, but they lived side by side. They didn't live together I understand, and Robert Wood was mostly raised up in his father's home, rather than his mother's. She must've been the housekeeper or whatever. And his father had been mayor of Natchez earlier anyway, so he probably influenced him.

Robert Wood was mayor and sheriff and postmaster. First he was elected mayor, but he ran for a second term and was defeated. Then he was made postmaster, and he stayed there until he was elected sheriff. Before that, as a young man, he worked as a printer for a printing company in Natchez, and this is how he and John R. Lynch got to be friends, because Lynch also worked as a printer.

None of this history is very well-known. It wasn't even discussed in school. I regret that I don't know enough of it. It was such a short period in history that the Reconstruction days occurred. And it was after this, in the early 1920s, that I was coming along, and, apparently, black people had kind of shied off from talking about it, since everything had all gone awry, you know. But they talked about Grandpa, and I can remember my mother saying Papa and Grandpa, but they didn't talk about his political life. They talked about it like I would talk about my daddy or you might talk about yours, without anything relating to his political life.

He died back out in Washington. He operated a store out there. I remember one of my relatives mentioned a great fire—that Washington had burned at one time, and the family had lost their property in the fire. I don't really know what the property was or anything, but I do know that his store has been torn down for the last twenty years. It was a brick store out in Washington. I remember that when we'd drive by there, my mother would say that was her grandfather's store.

Charles Harris and Selma Mackel Harris

Selma: I think when you are younger you don't pay attention to what the older people say. My dad was a great storyteller; he always set us down and told us about the families and different things that happened back then. But when you're younger, you don't have sense enough to record that or write it down for later years, you know, after they are gone. Then you are interested in it, as you get older.

Charles: Now the Maziques, they were a very, very wealthy family before the Civil War and afterward. They owned almost two-thirds of Adams County. A lot of it's been sold, but they were a very rich and powerful black family during that time.

Selma: And these people are related to us.

Charles: But they were all Baptists or Methodists and no Catholics, right?

Selma: Some of the Maziques are Catholics. My uncle married into the Mazique family. He married a Boyd whose people were Maziques, and that's how we knew their family, and some of them were Catholics. The Lees were Catholics, you know, and some of the Maziques are still.

Rayford Batieste

My grandmother, Rachel Batieste, lived to be, they say, a hundred and four years old. She was a baby in slavery. She used to walk around to the white families in the area where we lived in the country, and they would give her things—food, clothing—and she would carry it on top of her head. She'd have a big bundle, put it on top of her head, and carry it. She would walk from white family to white family. She would help them do the laundry. They would give her food in return, and I think that's how she survived back in those days before the government helped people.

She was light-skinned and short. I always remember her hair was short, but white. She was stout, and she walked with a stick three or four miles every day, and she was very active up until three weeks before she passed.

Marie Byrd Dennis

My great-grandfather's name was Richard Green. He became a doctor. He was from Fayette. All you have to do is go out there and say Green, and they'll start talking about him. They owned a plantation out there. It's just as you enter Fayette; there's a nice big pond sitting there. And Dr. Richard Green's father was owned; he was a slave.

I don't know if it's true or not, but my grandmother used to say that he was descended from an African chief. My mother always said that she was telling the truth, and I said, "Well, great!" You know, I didn't know Dr. Green because he died before I was born, but they said he was kind of a weird man. He didn't like for you to be cruel to animals or things like that, but my mama always said he could kind of predict the future, and I didn't believe in that because I just didn't believe it.

My grandmother told me one time that this man came riding up on a horse, and he was beating the dogs or something, and my great-grandfather told him, "Don't do that to an animal."

"I'll do what I want," the man said.

So my great-grandfather told him, "Well, go ahead, because before you get down the road, and the train whistle blows three times, you'll lose your head."

My grandmother said they all just looked at him because they thought he was kind of weird, too. The man went on down the road, and the train tracks were somewhere near, and they said before the whistle blew three times, the guy ran into a limb and cut his head off. That could be a fairy tale, and it could be the truth. I don't know. But it's what I heard.

My father used to say old Dr. Green was a witch doctor because, when we were talking about it one time, my dad says, "Well, he wasn't anything but an old witch doctor. You know that, don't you?" And I said, "No, I didn't." He said, "Well, that's what he was." I said, "Daddy, you don't believe that." He said, "So what? I believe in leprechauns." So you're bound to believe he was a witch doctor. But he was joking, I think. I hope he was.

Charles Harris, Sr.

None of my people have ever told me that any of my people was a slave, but I know my daddy, Hayes Harris, was a sharecropper because he got cheated out of all of his money. One year he made a good crop, and the next year he told Mama, "Well, I'm going to go out this year and make a big crop so I can have some for myself."

After everything, after he harvested the crop and gave it to the man, and he sold it—the man came with a book and said, "Hey, you did well this year. You come out even." So that's when he left the country and moved to town.

Today I am eighty years old, and I've never plowed a row or picked a row of cotton in my life.

Lettie Lewis

Now my mother and father were Catholics. My mother was Fannie Remus Hall, and my father was Richard Hall. She belonged to the Ladies' Auxiliary, and my father was a

Knight of St. Peter Claver. Well, naturally, I was baptized when I was a couple of months old or something. I was born on June 15, 1916.

My parents were Catholic, because my mother and her sister were raised by a white lady that lived here in Natchez, named Mrs. Eltringham. The girls had been born in Louisiana, and my grandmother let them come and live with this lady. Mrs. Eltringham was a Catholic, so she sent them to the Catholic schools, and that way, they were Catholics.

Somewhere in this house I've got my mother's marriage license. She and my father was married in 1890-something, but I don't know the exact date of that. My father used to dance this cakewalk or something. He even taught my oldest sister. At one time, she participated with him and danced at different functions. They used to dance at the hotels and balls and things like that, which the white citizens of Natchez was having. They would be featured dancers or something like that. They danced up at the Natchez Hotel. That was an old hotel; a part of it was where the Eola is now. They also used to dance at the American Legion Hall.

My parents were very active at Holy Family Church, but we would also sometimes go to St. Mary's Cathedral. They had nothing against you going to Cathedral to church if you wanted to. If we thought we were going to be late because we lived quite a distance from our church, we could go to Cathedral. If we missed a Mass, and that was a holy day of obligation or something, we could go to Cathedral because they had more masses than we had at Holy Family. I went there as a girl and continued since I've been grown.

They didn't have no special marked-off place for you to sit. That's one thing they never did, and the priests and nuns there would go and visit the sick, the black as well as the white, because they went to the Charity Hospital and things to visit, just as well as ours would. If they went to the hospital, whether they were black or white or whatever, they'd visit all of them, even people that were not Catholics.

David Montgomery

My grandmother, that was my daddy's mother, was an everyday churchgoer and everything, you know, the whole works there at Holy Family. Her name was Violet Montgomery. She was a seamstress in her young days. She used to make hoop-dresses and things like that for the people at pilgrimage. She also used to make queen gowns and things for the balls, you know; and she was, like I say, a good church person. Now, I can't go no farther back than her, you know.

My grandfather, David Montgomery, used to be a waiter at the Natchez Eola Hotel, and that's all I ever knew him to do, until he got where he couldn't work anymore. And he and my mother used to play the organ and the piano and everything in church. Daddy used to play the violin and guitar, too, and he used to go around in the joints and play when they didn't have jukeboxes and things. He could play all the old piano blues and stuff like that, but none of their kids could play instruments.

Aubrey Webb

I know that my mother was six years old when the first Holy Family Church was built. I do know that. I also know that the church cost less than $15,000 to be built. That's amazing. The architect was Ketteringham. But I never knew any of the crew members that worked on it originally, from when it was first built.

A lot of the men in my family were brickmasons and also in the family I married in, they're bricklayers. My mother-in-law's father, Minor Davis, played the violin at Cathedral. And I know that my mother, my mother-in-law, and Ms. Laura Allain, they attended Mass over at Cathedral before Holy Family was built. The first Holy Family Church building was built in 1894. That was on Beaumont Street. Eventually I bought the old church building on Beaumont that had been made into an apartment building. It was four apartments, and, let's see, I got $12 a month for the front apartment and for the side apartment, I got $10. But I didn't get it all the time. I still own that land now.

Chapter 4

School Days

Sidney Gibson

I started at St. Francis School, as it was called then, in 1938. I was in the fourth or the fifth grade. My family was Baptist. But during that time, I guess many black families were motivated to send their kids to Catholic school. It was said to be the best school in the county during that Jim Crow period when the black public schools were really treated second class.

Willie Fleming

I went to school at St. Francis from the early grades on, back in the 1930s. They sent a bus out through the country to pick up people and bring them into town to get a better education. We had the opportunity to go into the Natchez city school for black children. Some people did that, because the public school for blacks out in the country wasn't much. The teacher had too many kids to deal with. And it was a known fact that they'd get a better education at the Catholic school. But some of the people just wasn't able, I guess, to send their kids over there. You had to buy different clothes. You couldn't wear the kind of clothes you wore to school out in the country. Out there you could wear patches and go barefooted.

At St. Francis, there wasn't no code for dressing, but we wouldn't go over there barefooted. We had to buy shoes and a decent pair of pants and shirts, jackets. And the poor people back in the country, they couldn't afford that.

Wilbur Johnson

My parents were public school teachers over in Louisiana, and I guess they wanted to give me what was at that time considered the best educational opportunity for a black child in the area, and that was the Catholic school in Natchez. St. Francis was considered the best school because of the smaller number of students in the classroom, and the type of discipline that was involved, the religious aspect of it. Also, at that time, everything was segregated, and it was very seldom that blacks had a chance to have white teachers. So there was an opportunity to get educated with a variety of teachers. I guess at that time it was considered a privilege.

Barbara Washington

My mother and father were Baptist. My father was dead by this time, but my mother saw fit to send us to the Catholic school. I started in first grade. She knew it was a good school, and the priests and nuns cared for the black children. I'm sure that's the reason she sent us there. As children, they used to say that we thought we were better than others because we attended the Catholic school. That wasn't true, but it was a small circle of us who went to Catholic school, and we usually stayed within that circle. The children who attended Broomfield [the black public school] always liked to pick fights with us. They may have thought it was a privilege to attend the Catholic school, and maybe their parents couldn't afford it. I think it was like fifty cents a month at that time to attend school there. My mother was a maid, and she sacrificed to send us to St. Francis.

Joe Frazier

Many of the prominent black people in Natchez, even many that did not become Catholic, went to the Catholic school. The Catholic school educated a lot of the black people who made big contributions to this area, and not only in Natchez. We used to have buses coming from little towns close by, like Harrison and Fayette. And we had many children coming from the surrounding Louisiana areas—from Vidalia and Ferriday. So the school had a ripple effect. A lot of people were educated by the nuns and priests at St. Francis School. They may or may not have joined the faith, but they carried back a lot of the teaching and a lot of the education that was given here and made a contribution. A number of young people who went to St. Francis School went to college and became nurses and things, and then they came back to the community. They didn't all stay, but a lot of them came back for a while. And we used to look up to them because they went to Catholic school.

Joe Hall

The Sisters treated us very well. Most of them were pretty strict. We had one, our principal at the time, Sister Norbert, who was very strict, but she was also very fair, you know. She had no picks and chooses, and children knew that. You could feel it. They respected her, and everybody liked her—no ifs, ands, or buts about it. They really did. I guess it was because she was fair. It didn't matter if she was so strict, you know, as long as it was equal treatment of everybody. Sister Norbert also coached the girls' basketball team, and they always won.

Vernon Williams

Yeah, Sister Norbert coached the girl's team when I was in high school. She'd be down on the sidelines in her habit. She was the coach, boss, dictator, and everything. She hated to lose. She would really deal them out, man. "You didn't play your best. You didn't do your best." She was like Bobby Knight—maybe not as radical—but she went out there every day to win. She had some good players, too, very good.

Julia Davis

I just loved the teachers and the nuns, and the way they taught. They were very, very strict. When they tell you to do something, you better do it, or you got a whipping. I think it was Sister Norbert who had a broomstick, and you had to put your hand out there, and she would hit you about five or six times across your hand. When she told you to do something, then you did it. It was discipline. We don't have it today.

My favorite was Sister Catherine. She taught me when I was in the eighth grade. She always made you feel like you were at home. If I didn't understand something, she would take her time, sit down, and talk to me. I was always shy, and she would always tell me, "You can do anything you want to do. Just apply yourself." She always gave us a chance.

People respected the nuns back in that time, because of their teaching, and the way they carried themselves spiritually. When you'd see them, they would be praying or saying the Rosary. They tried to help others. We were considered poor, but there were some poorer than us, and anything that they could share with us, they did. People donated clothes or anything to them, and they would give it to children in need. Fed them, too.

Lavera Gibson Allen

After graduating from St. Francis, I went to Houston to Texas Southern University. There were twenty-three of us in my graduating class, and twelve of us went to college. And since then I know that three more went to community college. The Sisters told us how to go to the library and pull the books to research the schools that we wanted. They helped us fill out the financial-aid papers. They gave us lists of scholarships and grants and, you know, companies like Pepsi-Cola and Coca-Cola that offered partial scholarships or this type of thing. They really pushed us to do our best where the ACT test was concerned.

Sister Edna even took the girls and had a session about going off from home, and how we had to be not only young ladies, but young mothers because we had to play the role of taking care of ourselves, making sure the feminine hygiene and all that was taken care of and preparing ourselves for making sound decisions, and how to say no to the boys. They were always there for us.

Willie Fleming

Everybody who went to Catholic school had to participate in everything at the school. During Lent, everybody would go up in the church for Stations of the Cross. Everybody did the same thing, whether you were Catholic or non-Catholic. I guess being a Catholic helped in a lot of ways. The Sisters took better care of you when you were Catholic. They'd look out for the Catholics, better than they would for the non-Catholics. And the Sisters was always after them about getting baptized, getting baptized. I just decided to go ahead and get baptized, so they wouldn't be nagging me no more. The Sisters taught religion all day if they had the opportunity. We had one Sister, when I was in seventh and eighth grades, and she would forget about the other subjects if you got her stirred up on religion. Her name was Sister Eustochium. She'd just talk a whole half hour into another period. She loved talking about religion.

Lavera Gibson Allen

I really grew up in the Catholic Church. I'm Baptist by denomination. My home church growing up was Pleasant Green Baptist. But I went to St. Francis School from kindergarten all the way through. Both of my sisters went there, too. So, of course, we were part of all the teachings and everything that went along with the church because we were involved in the school. We were a part of First Friday Mass, you know, the fasting on Fridays until twelve noon. It was something you grew up with, so it became a habit. It became a part of you. But I stayed Baptist. I never joined the Catholic Church. There was never any pressure to become Catholic at school. I don't remember any. They expected us to follow the rules, to learn the lessons. The invitation was always there without it being said that you should belong, you know. It was not something that was forced upon you.

Mary Cecealia Lee

The Sisters were trying to mold us in the way of the Lord, and they did that, believe me. We had to wear long skirts. We had one Sister—Sister Sacred Heart she was called—who would check the length of your dress and, if it wasn't where she wanted it to be, she would take the hem out of your skirt in front of everybody in the class. I saw her do that. So the best thing for you to do was wear a long skirt. Here I was wearing hand-me-downs from white people. My mother would be buying clothes from them for small amounts, you know, and everything that I had was maybe not the length that Sister wanted it, but I would go home and fix it and press it, so it would be long enough.

Mazie Belle Rolax

My two brothers and I came into the church in the 1920s. We were in Catholic school all our life, and this is the only church we've ever been to, but I think we was baptized when we was about seven. My little brother was the first one that became Catholic. He was baptized when he was six. Eventually the whole family converted. The children came in first, and then Mama came in, and then Daddy because we felt that the family should all be together, you know.

A lot of the children at the school became Catholic because they loved the Sisters and the priests. Some more, I think, must have come while they were in school, and then they went back to the other religions. I remember W. D. Washington. He was a class ahead of me. He went to Catholic school all the time, and he did everything we did but go to communion. He sang in the choir. He was in everything, and that's the way it was in those days. You did everything the Catholics did but go to communion. You loved the whole thing.

We had Mass every morning during Lent, and we didn't mind it at all. We were running like everything. We went to Mass at seven o'clock, went back home and had breakfast and ran back to school, to be back to school before nine o'clock. We ran, and none of that was a problem; it was a pleasure really. You were getting your gold stars and your spiritual bouquets and all that, and that went on your report card.

Wilbur Johnson

Dealing with the nuns had a tremendous effect upon me. It helped break down that color barrier. It created an experience for me. I remember that the nuns used to send me and a friend of mine to go to pay bills. This friend had a light complexion, and one time when we went to pay a bill, this lady wouldn't talk to me; she had a preference to talk to my friend, and I felt it was because of his complexion. I had the money, but every time I would try to say something to her, she would shrug me off to talk to him. At school I never had to experience that. I knew that there was a difference out in the community because it was obvious. But at school there was a love shown to us that made us feel secure.

However, I did have one experience, around seventh grade, with a nun who, for some reason, had a peculiar attitude. We had a feeling that she thought we were filthy or dirty because every time she would touch us, or we got close to her, she had to clean her hands. At that time, we didn't really understand the implication. We just took her as being someone to amuse us. Other than that, I can't remember any instance where anyone indicated or said or acted in any way because of color at St. Francis. There were favorites; some of them were light-skinned and some of them were dark-skinned. I guess it depended upon the teacher or nun. But I would say, other than that one instance, I can't think of any experience of favoritism because of color.

Barbara Washington

We had some white neighbors when I was growing up, but I didn't look at them as being white. I knew they were different, but I really never paid any attention to a person's color, only the ways they were treating me and as a human being. From childhood on up, I demanded that; I was going to respect them, and they would respect me. I guess I got that from going to the Catholic school because all that "yes, sir," and "no, ma'am," and all this to the white people, we never did do that. Father Gaudette taught us to say, "yes, Mrs. so-and-so," or "no, Mrs. so-and-so," or whatever; Not "yes ma'am" and "no ma'am." At school we'd say, "Yes, Sister so-and-so." But it never was a "yes, ma'am." The priests and nuns were white, and they were friends of ours, truly good friends. So we looked at everybody else the same way.

Vernon Williams

I left the public school in 1938 and went down to St. Francis. And during that same year, I was baptized by Father

John Mulkeen. I was fourteen years old. My brother had already been going to St. Francis, and he actually was the one who got me to be a Catholic. He said, "It's good, man. Come on and join." I had been going to church with him long before I was a Catholic. I would go to masses with him and go to the benedictions and what-not. And I liked it so well.

Father Mulkeen was a fine one. He was a character, man. He was short—Santa Clauslike—kind of pudgy, and just as red-cheeked, red nose, Irish as he could be, with an Irish accent. I had a habit of sneaking up the hall and going around the school peeping in the windows of the different classrooms, and he caught me. He said, "I'll tell you this, Vernon Williams. If you don't get out of that hallway, I'll put my foot on you."

In those days one of the priests was the religion instructor. He would also come over every month and read your report card. You can imagine what that would be like now. He would come into each classroom. The Sister would have the report cards all stacked up, and he'd come in, call your name, and read your marks off out loud to everybody. Naturally, you wanted to do good because you'd want everybody else to know.

Joe Hall

Father Gaudette was our basketball coach when I was in school, and we were so-so. We won our share. Now Father Gaudette was a real good guy. He was talented, and he was real tough. He'd go up side your head. He could wrestle, and he could sing. He was an excellent musician, and he'd show you his temper. We had a glee club, and I think it was a real good glee club. We traveled through Louisiana and places raising money for the school. We also sang at Mass, and right during church service, if we would get off key or something, he'd bang down on the organ—right in church, in the middle of Mass—bam, and start over. He was something.

And when we built the high school, he'd get right out there and take his shirt off and help you dig the ditch. I'm serious. We helped build that high school. Father Gaudette built it partly with hired labor and partly donated labor. Men from the parish donated some time, but some of them had skills that they made their living with, so, naturally, they were paid. They worked every day, like laying the bricks and things. But for digging the trenches for the foundation, Father Gaudette had schoolboys, the high school boys. We'd go out and do that, and he'd get down in there with us. When they started building the high school, he set up a schedule where the boys would work. I think we would have one day a week that we missed from school, and we would have to go and work building the school.

Now, after I got to be a grown man, I heard Father William Morrissey criticize Father Gaudette. He thought that it was criminal what Father Gaudette did, taking us out of school. I can understand where he was coming from. He felt it wasn't right to take kids away from their education, but, in my opinion, it was an education. I told him that when Father Gaudette took me out there to work, he took me out of the poolroom. I wasn't going to be at school anyway. I didn't lose anything. I gained from it. When you help to build something, you just feel a great part of it, and I think it did that for a lot of guys in my time. They felt a part of the place.

Chapter 5

Color Lines

Elsie Jackson

Nellie Jackson—my grandmother used to tell me about her. She used to come and visit all the time because my grandmother had five girls. My mother would say, well, she was looking for girls for her services. Nellie Jackson ran a house of ill repute. She would visit my grandmother, come on Sunday and sit and talk and tell her how beautiful her girls were, and this and that. But my grandmother, not being a dummy, could see through it, so, finally, Nellie Jackson stopped coming.

Nellie Jackson had moved here from Louisiana, I think. She was one of those high-yellow ladies, too. She was a big one, but she was a very attractive woman. Yes, she was. She was a parishioner of the church, too—Holy Family Church. She came on Sunday with all her girls. Yeah, they advertised every Sunday. And she was a good contributor. She was nice to the priests and nice to the Sisters. Christmas and different holidays, she'd bring gifts. She was a very kindhearted person. But she wasn't buried from our church. When she died, she was buried from St. Mary's, and she left her money there, too.

The customers at her house were all white, and in the old days her workers were just blacks. Later on she had black and white girls. Everybody knew about her, because this is where everybody took their young sons and things. Nellie was it. She ran the town. She ran the town because her information ran the town. She had them all. Anything downtown that had a suit on, she had it. Even the wives respected Nellie, but none of our black people could go there. Our black men couldn't go there. That was a no-no for them.

Marie Byrd Dennis

My grandfather on my mother's side was Charles O'Neil. He was an Irish Catholic, who settled in Fayette, Mississippi, and married my grandmother, Annie Laurel Green. They were not actually married. You know, back then, black and white didn't really marry, but they lived together. So that was my mother's mother. She was a fairly big woman, and she was Baptist. I do know that. She was one of those hard-shell Baptists, but when my mom was born, she gave my mom to her sister because her sister couldn't have children. Her sister's name was Emma Green, and that's the one I really call my grandmother. She raised my mom up in the Catholic religion. She was Baptist herself, but she raised her up as Catholic. That's kind of strange, but she did. She sent her to school at St. Francis. Matter of fact, she raised my mom's sister and brother up as Catholics, too. She just always said that she felt that that was the right way that things should be.

I met my grandfather, Charles O'Neil, once about a year before he died. He was a tall man, blue eyes, and you could tell his hair had been blondlike, and—from the time that I met him—he had a very sweet disposition. He lived in Fayette all his life. He had a grocery store there, and he went to the Catholic church there. That time I met him, he was arguing with my mom—his daughter—about not letting him know about us. She just said, "Well, I didn't think you wanted to know." He knew who she had married and everything, but he had never met us—his grandchildren—and he was upset with her about that.

Now on my father's side, he had a sister named Lena, and she married a man named Fields. They called him Bubba. I think his name was Mike. He was white. They were married at Holy Family Church, either in the chapel or in the church. I can't remember, but it was like a secret wedding at that time. It happened in the early 1960s. He was a member of St. Mary's parish. My mom was a witness to the wedding.

They had lived together for years and had three children before they were married. I'd always visit them. They seemed pretty happy. They weren't really quiet about their relationship. They just went and came like they wanted to. He would come down the street and go into the house. I don't think they ever went out together anywhere because the black people knew Lena, and the whites, I don't know whether they knew what Lena was or not. If I was to see her, I couldn't tell what she was. Lena looked Italian. She had long, black hair, brown eyes, very fair complexion, but kind of what you call olive fair. She looked more Italian than she did anything. People who knew her considered her as black. People who didn't, thought she was white. Bubba Fields' family knew she was black. His mother was very bitter against Lena. She wanted to take her kids and raise them and let her go, but Lena wouldn't go along, and Bubba wouldn't let her do it either.

Finally he took Lena away from here, so they could live better. They moved to Las Vegas. Bubba was a gambler. He gambled for a living. So they moved out there.

Mary Cecealia Lee

My aunt, Arolia, had six boys by a white fellow that couldn't marry her. His name was Buddy Davis. He never had a white wife, and he was with her the whole while to raise those kids. This was here in Natchez, I guess in the 1920s or '30s. His family had a meat market, or some kind of business, downtown.

They lived together as man and wife on a little side street off St. Catherine's. It was an African American neighborhood, and all Buddy's children went to St. Francis School. And they were members of Holy Family. Altar boys, you name it. I don't know whether Buddy was Catholic or not, but he made sure that those boys went there, and he was financing everything. He even helped feed us. He was a very kind man. Used to wear a cowboy hat all the time, and I think he would be on a horse sometimes.

There were times that my aunt told me about, when there was a kind of upheaval, and the word would go around that all the black women that were going with white men would have to leave town. Then Buddy would have to get her out of here in the wee hours of the morning. She'd go off to Tennessee, or wherever her other sisters were, until things quieted down. But they were accepted in the black community just fine, no problem.

Mamie Mazique

My cousin, Elizabeth—we called her Baby—she was a light-skinned woman, and she was married to a white man. His name was Peter Burns. His family owned the Burns Shoestore uptown. They lived right next door to us, and we didn't think anything about it. Her name was Elizabeth Stampley Burns. This was back in the 1940s. I don't know where they were married. I have heard that they went to Chicago and got married, but I don't know that.

They lived openly in the black community. I don't suppose they were so open among the whites because there was nobody to associate with them. I don't know about his people. I don't even know how much his people associated with them, but I know he was open in the black community. He would get up in the morning after breakfast and stand on the corner and a cab would pick him up and take him to the shoestore, so he wasn't hidden.

He and Elizabeth rode in cars, traveled, went to the country, and went out riding on Sunday. Nobody bothered them. I can remember being at their house so much because we was right next door to each other. Never heard anybody making crazy prank calls on the phone or stuff like that. They had a very normal life as far as I could see, and their kids also.

They had two boys, Charles Burns and James Burns. James is dead. He went to the army, and then retired from the army and stayed up in New York. He died up there. Charles is still living. He's living in New Orleans. Charles did a lot of photography work. He graduated from Southern University, and then he went to work at Southern. He retired from there and ended up staying in Louisiana, but he's been back and forth up here to Natchez. He's married to a young lady, and they live in New Orleans.

I had a sister who was a registered nurse. She wasn't married, and I know she dated white fellows. I just never thought anything about that. I have another sister who had a son, and his father was white. My mother was—what, three-quarters? Almost white, you know. We never paid any attention to color, and we never made any exceptions. It was nothing big in our life, and we treated each other nice. I think that it's a way you can carry yourself, and they carry themselves, and you can respect each other. We went where we wanted to. We wasn't white, and we knew that, but we had white friends, and we had plenty of black friends.

Rayford Batieste

I used to do some brick work for an African American man named Stevenson. He had his own crew. When he'd get a job as a subcontracting bricklayer, then he would go to work, and I would say he got a job every week. He built chimneys and brick walls. I mostly helped him build chimneys. At that time, most people were burning wood for heat. They didn't have any gas. Most of the jobs that I helped him on were out in the country. He couldn't get his regular men on Saturday. They'd drink a little bit, and, you couldn't get them to go out, so that gave me a chance to go out with him. I'd go out and be an apprentice for him.

At that time, I don't think there was very many crew leaders who were African American. I think Mr. Stevenson was about the only one. There was other bricklayers, but I don't think any of them could just go out and subcontract a job like he did. There's some more now who I think came up under him and become contractors, subcontractors, masonry contractors.

Mr. Stevenson came up in a family where most of them was masons and bricklayers, but for him to get the chance to subcontract—well, I have some thoughts about it. For one thing, you couldn't tell that he was a real African American.

He was very light-skinned. Back then, I think, the whites was a little more liberal toward the lighter African Americans.

There was some of that in Holy Family Church. I feel sometimes that the nuns and priests, most of them white, would be a little more comfortable with the lighter-skinned ones, and cater to them a little more, but that changed in later years.

Black people would get together, and they would joke about it. They really would. I used to hear it all the time in the community. You'd get in a little group or you'd be out maybe at a picnic, and they'd start talking about the Catholics. The Baptists would say, "Well, you know, they don't like black people. They like the lighter ones." And, "They lean toward the lighter ones," and, "They don't care very much about black people in that church, dark-skinned ones." You'd hear that pretty often. That happened years ago. I don't think that's true today.

Elsie Jackson

We were aware of skin shades when I was in school. That was around the time it had started to darken. But the older group, the ones maybe three or four years ahead of me, they were light. They had one or two mixed in there, but overall they were light. And then, as the years would go by, you'd get two or three more, and that sort of faded out most of the light-skinned people. Eventually you had more dark people than light-skinned people.

But we were definitely treated differently when I was in school. I was black, and they were white—even with the nuns and the priests. They didn't do anything wrong, but you could see a difference. Why is that person always picked on?

Why is she always doing something? I might have had some little rap-taps on my head. She maybe had long hair, and I might have had more brains, and she might not have any to show. See, this is what it was like.

But it all changed because the lighter-skinned women were marrying the darker men. That's what happened. My grandmother, you know, some of her kids were light, and some were dark. But she was kind of brown, not too brown, light, with long Indianlike hair. Then, she married my grandfather, and he was the color of that radio; he was black. So what can come from that? You can look at the school over there now and see my little granddaughter, Keishawn. I have a mixture of grandchildren, but Keishawn has red hair, long, red hair. But her brother is black because the dad's dark. See, that's what makes the difference. I have one grandson, and where he would come from, I don't know. He has green eyes, and he's very light. His hair is redder than Keishawn's, and his mama's dark. My husband was dark. He wasn't black, black, but he was dark and look at my daughter, Darlene, Keishawn's mother; she's very light. She's lighter than Keishawn. See, this is the way it happens. You know, the genes may pick up something from way back.

Duncan Morgan

A lot of the students at our school early on were the ones whose father was a relatively wealthy white person, and he would want his children to have an education. There was no such thing as decent public school, so they sent them to the school in the basement of Cathedral, and later on the school here—St. Francis, later Holy Family. And the children were exposed to the church and joined. In fact, I've heard people say that, around the turn of the century, there may have been three families in the parish that were of dark complexion. All the rest were mixed.

That changed gradually. If you look at pictures, I suspect, from the 1920s, you would see more light complexions than dark. Then Father Mulroney was here in the late '30s and early '40s, and he got a lot of converts. He was generations ahead of his time. He went out through the country, talking to everybody, preaching in the Baptist churches and all, and his style was loud and forceful, and he got many converts. And then the school—more and more people were coming into the school, and the children would wind up getting baptized before they graduated—probably 80 percent of them. Half of those would drift away, but many of them stayed, so it was a gradual thing that occurred between the '20s and the '40s.

Today the church is well-assimilated. It would probably be a shock if anybody tied that in now with the present congregation. It's just something that nobody would ever think of. If anything distinguishes the church, it may be education. Many of the parishioners are relatively well-educated, people who have either pulled themselves up or have risen. There are a good many teachers and middle-class people. Probably some of the best parishioners are still at the low end of the financial stratum. If there is any distinction, it would be more along those lines than purely racial or mixture of skin color.

Another thing about Natchez is that until just after World War II, housing was the most integrated part of Natchez. This house right on the corner here, for instance, is white. As far back as I can remember, white people have lived there. The house right behind it is black. Any street that you went down, even with the big mansions, right behind it, on the next street, or a lane or an alley behind it, had tenement houses where there were black people. Anywhere you could go, it was like that. There may have been a millionaire's house with four or five two-room cabins behind it.

There was a general mix. Not that there was any social equality or anything, but there were, in some parts of town, people of the same economic level who were mixed in maybe one or two white families here and three or four black ones there. Their families had been there for generations, and they got along. The children played together. In a place like this, before the general civil rights explosion, there were individual relationships. They might turn their nose up at the masses. But if you were somebody that I had known for generations, if you had worked for me for a long time and all, you were as close to me as a sister or brother. Some people may have felt, well, "That's my nigger." So, there was the individual relationship; it was paternalistic, true, but it was there.

Barbara Washington

Right where we lived, we were in between two white families—the Martins and the Cooks—and they were like family to us. They had children, and we grew up together, and we fought together, we did; we grew up just like if it was another family. And my growing up days was good. But I can remember one time we were going down to St. Catherine Creek, down Liberty Road. It was two of my sisters, myself, and two or three white girls that lived along in there. And we were just having fun, you know, going along, and the next thing we know, the police had us in the car. And we were kids. We was very young, but they didn't put us in jail. They called our parents to come get us. On our way there, they told us, didn't we know that we shouldn't be walking and playing with those white girls the way we were doing. And so we told them, no, they were next-door neighbors. The white girls' parents went down to the police station and let the police have it with both barrels. They didn't bother us anymore.

You know, I didn't look at my neighbors as being white. I knew they were different, but I really never paid any attention to a person's color. There were all kinds of people around me, and we all was friends, you know. I never was surrounded with hate. I always felt love.

Ora Frazier

I remember I went to Laurel, Mississippi, before Frazier and I were married, and I went to this store. There was a white man there from an old family, and he asked me what I was doing. I told him I was teaching school, but I was going to get married soon. I knew this man was Catholic, and I said, "I'm marrying a Catholic guy." He said, "You are? Well, you got to come on in the church, you know."

This was his thing. He said, "We don't care who comes to our church. You know, black people and white people come." At the time, I didn't know any black Catholics in Laurel. He said, "We have black people and white people come to our church, and we don't have any problem with this." This was in 1958. And he said, "I'm glad you're marrying a Catholic guy 'cause I know you got a good man." It seemed like everybody had a little greater respect for black Catholics, you know, Catholics period, but most especially black Catholics. You must be something else if you got two strikes against you—you're black and you're Catholic, you know. He said, "You're marrying a good guy. You can always come to our church. When you bring him, you can come to our church." And he emphasized that. I said, "Okay, I'll do that."

So there was something that sort of separated the Catholics from non-Catholics in terms of black and white. I had never thought about that until then, but he emphasized that. That was 1958, long before any civil rights in Mississippi.

Aubrey Webb

There were quite a few whites that came to Mass at Holy Family. There was Ms. Annie McManiqual and Ms. Hattie Marron. They had a hat store downtown, Hamilton-Marron Hat Store, and Miss Dotty; she was there all the time. And the lady right up here on Rankin Street by the name of Ms. Blanche Fields; she has a lovely family. She's dead now. There was Ms. Carrigan; she had the Natchez Fish Market. She was here all the time; she and Ms. Annie Marron. Ms. Annie McManiqual was from Philadelphia, but Ms. Annie [Hattie] Marron was from here, and Ms. Carrigan was from here. They were members at Cathedral, but we were tickled to death for them to come because they helped our parish out.

They were people who just weren't prejudiced at all, but, back in those days, they'd say you were being a nigger-lover or something, so they had to be careful. But they didn't care who knew they came over here to Mass. They would sit in the back, and the priest would move them up in the front. He'd tell me when you come here, you don't sit in the back;

you sit in the front. Then, that way, he said, I won't have to be hollering too loud.

Mazie Belle Rolax

We used to go to Cathedral, but you sat on the last seats all the time, maybe two benches in the back or something. I remember there was one Lent we had to go there; we was making those forty days, and there was an old lady there with three or four kids, and she kept getting up and moving them right during Mass. And we'd have to move to stay behind her. The seats weren't marked, but you just knew in those days. No matter where you went, if there were white people there, you automatically sat in the back whether there was a sign or not.

We did have whites, though, that came to our church. I remember the Passbachs came out and the Tucchios; I think they came, too. There were the Mascagnis. They always sat in the back all the time, three or four back seats. There was a lot of them that came practically every Sunday. They would always come to seven o'clock Mass or whatever, and they always left before the final blessing. I remember Father Gaudette got so mad when they left before the last blessing. And I remember when he turned around and said, "Don't come if you can't stay."

Lettie Lewis

It was no problem with us going to Cathedral because if we were going to be late for church and coming from across town, then we could go to Cathedral. They never didn't want you to come there because you were black, or anything like that. Until they started the integration stuff, we used to have a lot of white Catholics that came to our Mass at Holy Family. A lot of them lived on St. Catherine Street, and they would come right there to our church to Mass every Sunday. There was the Stallones; they had a plumbing business. And there was the Sam Anzelone family that had a grocery store. There was a lady named Miss Julia. I can't think of what her last name was. The Veruccis....They would just come in the church and sit anywhere. They came to different things that we would have. The last time I went to the church they had this musical extravaganza, a concert for different choirs and things; there were some of them there then. I saw Buck Verucci; he used to be a plumber. He was friends with my husband because they were raised up right close together off of St. Catherine. He used to do some plumbing for us. I told him, "We have got old now." He was walking with a stick, and so was I.

Chapter 6

Faith and Family

Eugene Dottery

If there was any way possible, people would try to send their children to the Catholic school, because the teachers would take so much more pains with them. And, of course, if the children go to Catholic school, eventually, a large percent of them will become Catholic. That keeps the church going. They get a lot of members from children going to the school and becoming Catholics on their own. A lot of them don't do it until they leave home, but they eventually do because they get that training in them.

When I was young, I lived not too far from the Catholic school, and some of the boys I knew were going to the school. But what really got me started was later when a guy in the neighborhood got shot. People said that very week the Sisters had come begging this guy to come back to church. Now I don't know whether he went back or not, but that kind of got me to thinking. From then on, I kind of had a leaning toward the Catholic Church, but it was years before I became Catholic.

I was about twenty-three or so when my wife and I were baptized. Until then I didn't belong to a church. I'd go to different churches. It didn't matter. Just wherever the crowd went, I'd go, until I finally decided to join the Catholic Church. Before I'd even been to a Catholic church, just from observing the people and hearing them talk, and observing the churches I had been to, I realized that the Catholic Church was what I wanted.

In those other churches, a lot of the pastors, to my way of thinking, were hypocrites. They preached good sermons, but most of them didn't live good lives. That was one of the main things. And the Catholics just seemed like nicer people on the whole. Then, you notice how the pastor and the Sisters was around among the people, seeing after them. That made a big difference. In fact, believe it or not—it's a shame—but there were some people, when they got old and started going down, they'd try to join the Catholic Church because they knew they'd be taken care of. They realized that these people were more sympathetic. That's another one of the reasons I became Catholic.

I heard a lot of criticism about becoming Catholic. A lot of people had the wrong idea about the church. They'd say we was worshiping statues, idol worshippers, we pray to the priest, a lot of things like that. Of course, as the years went by, gradually things began to change, and nowadays they don't look at the Catholic Church that way.

After I was Catholic, this one cousin of mine said, "You'd be okay if you just got some religion." He was beginning to see the things in me that I'd seen in the average Catholic before I joined. But he was worried because I hadn't got religion. He said, "It's all right to belong to this Catholic Church, but get some religion."

He meant getting religion like the Baptists used to do. They'd have to go off and pray until they see something. Sometimes they prayed for weeks, constantly, and then, all at once, I don't know if they'd have a dream or what, but they'd say that they see things. Or they might ask God to prove to them that they got religion by letting them see the sun shower or something. They come out with a feeling that God is after them, which he probably was. To me, that wasn't necessary. But my cousin thought that it was. And since I hadn't done that, he didn't think I was saved.

Barbara Washington

At age thirteen, I decided to be baptized and join the Catholic Church. With my mother being Baptist, naturally I had attended some Baptist churches. I tried becoming a Baptist twice. At eleven years old, I got on the Mourners' Bench, that's what they called it in the Baptist church, to try and get religion. But I didn't see anything like what my grandmother had told me you would. She always told me that you would feel something and you would know something. So when I was on the Mourner's Bench, I prayed to see my father. I prayed real hard because my dad died when I was a baby. I wanted to see him so, but I didn't see him.

At age twelve, I got on the Mourners' Bench again at Pleasant Green Baptist Church, and I didn't see or feel anything like what the Baptists say you must do. At that time, I made up my mind to become Catholic, and I started taking instruction at the Catholic school. Then, during the time I was taking instructions—it was on a Saturday morning—I saw my father. Then I knew without a doubt that I had religion because I had never seen him when he was alive, but I knew that it was him. It was in a dream, that's true, but after the dream I woke up, and I went and told Mama that I had religion. Since I hadn't been going to the Baptist church, she just thought I was dreaming, but I did see my dad. It was something that I knew within myself, and I knew that I had to be baptized. My mother didn't want it, but I was determined. I wanted to be a Christian, so I just made my mind up and got baptized in the Catholic Church on Easter Saturday in 1949. I received my first holy communion that Easter Sunday.

There were about fifteen of us who got baptized, and it was just beautiful. I felt like a saint. I felt really good, and I knew that I was in touch with God. It was a beautiful experience. I felt like a different person because I actually prayed. I wanted to be a better person. I wanted to be a good person, and I actually prayed.

They say that we just go up to the Catholic church and worship the statues, but in my case that was not true.

Vernon Williams

All my life I've heard people say things about the Catholic Church. They'll say, man, you go down there, and you got to confess to the priest and things like that. It don't matter. It wasn't embarrassing to me to hear that. Sometimes I wouldn't say anything back; sometimes I might have said something I can't tell you right now.

I was baptized by Father Mulroney. They called Father Mulroney the Baptizer. He had so many converts. He had converts all over. He was a saintly acting man. And he didn't mind coming where you were. I don't care where it was.

I remember one day he was supposed to go up to a program at St. Joseph, Louisiana, and he asked me to drive him over there. They had asked him up there to speak. It was some program for black youth. They had built a playground, and he was supposed to take part in the ceremony. They got up there, and they had about seven or eight Baptist preachers on the stage. I think Father Mulroney was the only white up there, and everybody made his speech, but nobody ever called on Father Mulroney. I was right at the stage that day, and I pulled this guy's coattail and said, "Hey, Father Mulroney has a speech."

So the guy said, "Oh, yeah, we almost forgot about the Father here." Just ignoring him; that's what they were trying to do. The guy pulled his watch out and said, "We'll give the Father two minutes here to say something." He got up, man, he began to speak; he was throwing fire. His speech was so fine that people were clapping. Finally, the guy wanted to shut him up, and the people said, "No, let him talk. Let him talk!"

I enjoyed it myself.

Julia Davis

I didn't become a Catholic until I was about twenty-one or twenty-two in the late 1950s. Going to Catholic school, I'd always dreamed of being a Catholic, but my mother wanted me to be a Baptist, so I would go to church with her. But I was used to doing what all the Catholics did; that was what I wanted.

Later on in life, I would go to church every once in a while, but I wasn't real active. You see, I had some hard days in my life. I went and found out most things for myself the wrong way. My mother was very strict, but she never would talk to us about things that young ladies should know. So I lived a kind of fast life.

There wasn't much good happening around me. And I said to myself, it's time for me to stop and do something constructive with my life. I don't want to lose my soul and go to hell. So this made me turn around. I decided that I wanted to become a Christian, and I started praying. I read the Bible, and I started praying. When I was praying, I was almost in a trance. It was like I was in this world by myself. I would pray, and I could hear people talking around me, but it was like they weren't even there. I would have dreams, strange dreams—like I was talking to God, and I was in a place of nothing but beauty. The trees and everything had changed, like it was a new world to me.

I knew that something good was happening in my life. So I came over and talked to Father, and I told him the things that I had seen and how I had prayed, and that it was time for a change in my life. I told him that I wanted to be a Catholic, and I took instructions in the Catholic faith and was baptized.

At that time, I had two children, and I wasn't married, so I had my two children baptized, and, from then on, my family was Catholic. I made that change in my life, and I've been trying to stay in that change ever since.

My family couldn't believe I was going to be a Catholic because all of them are either Baptists or Methodists. But I said, "I have made up my mind what I want to be. This is where my family's going. When they get to be adults, if they want to change and go into another church, that's up to them. But I brought them up as Catholics, and so far all of them are still Catholics, and their families are Catholics.

Some people say, "Well, Catholics never pray." I say, "You're wrong." I pray every day. In my work, I pray. I do home health-care work, so I know that I'm doing something useful, and, when I'm helping somebody else, I can tell them to pray because God is there for you. All you got to do is ask him. I know that to be true, and I feel good when I can go in a patient's home and get them a bath or help them to do the things that they can't do for themselves, and even if it's just to say a prayer. I know I did something good. It just fills me up.

Margie Hoggatt

I couldn't trade my religion for any other religion. I love being a Catholic. It just means everything to me. I have children who joined other churches, and that worried me at first. Then I talked to a priest about it, and he said, "Don't worry about that. When your children get grown, they're free to make their own choices. You raised them and did all you could, but if they decide to join other churches, let them do it. Don't worry about it." So I stopped worrying about it, but I told them I'm going to stay a Catholic until I die.

My son doesn't believe in the way they baptize at the Catholic church. He says, "Mama, the Bible say you're supposed to be immersed in the water, and they just sprinkle you or pour water over your head." He said, "I don't want you to be lost, Mama."

I said, "How am I going to be lost?"

"Because you wasn't immersed in the water." He thinks that. The Church of Christ that he belongs to now believes you're supposed to be immersed in the water to be saved.

I say that the Bible says one baptism, and I've been baptized. I don't need another. That's what I tell my son. He wants me to think that, with the baptism I got, I won't be saved.

Lavera Gibson Allen

At school, I went through the ritual of saying the Rosary and studying catechism just as if I were Catholic. And

I can remember when I was in the seventh grade, I wanted to be a Catholic. My boyfriend, Robert, was studying to be baptized. I thought, "I'm going to die if I don't become Catholic." I remember going home and telling Mama, "Everybody in my class is a Catholic."

Mama said, "That's no reason to be a Catholic, sweetheart." I had already been baptized a Baptist. She said, "Change your faith if it's something that you really have to do, but not because of your friends." She also said, "God is going to be the same regardless of your denomination."

But I felt that if they didn't let me be a Catholic, I was not going to survive the rest of the school year. Of course, I did survive, and, by the time I got to eighth grade, everything was fine. And I stayed Baptist. Still today, on Ash Wednesday, I'm there at the Catholic church. During the Lent season, I'm fasting. It's something that I learned and I like it, and I want to do it.

I had a couple of friends, this past Lent, say, "Wash your face. You got ashes on your face." And I said, "That's because I went to Mass this morning and it's Ash Wednesday." It amazes me that people don't know the custom. So they look and wonder why, knowing that I'm a Baptist.

One of my girlfriends said to me, "You still do the rituals, huh?"

And I said, "Yeah, because they mean something."

Lucille Royal Mackel

I grew up in a Catholic family in New Orleans, and as a matter of fact I was engaged to a guy down there, but he was sent overseas in the service. This was during World War II. I was working on a defense job, and I went to my girlfriend's house to find out about my boyfriend. There was a friend of his who had just come back from overseas, and I was trying to find out if he had any news. I got there and my girlfriend introduced me to Sergeant Mackel. He had been overseas something like four years and nine months.

When he met me, he said, "Can I drive you home?" and I said, "No, because I live right around the corner."

He said, "Well, can I walk you home?"

I said, "Well, I guess so." So he walked me home, and my mother came to the door. Mother came and got his pedigree, and she kept saying, "That soldier is married." But I found out through friends in town that he wasn't married. We courted about nine months, and decided to get married. Mama wanted me to have this big church wedding, and in those days to do that Bob had to turn Catholic. So we went and talked to the priest, and Bob told him he belonged to the Masons.

The priest said, "Well, you cannot marry in the church because you're a Mason."

Bob said, "Well, I'm not going to change."

That upset the family so bad and, finally, the priest said, "Well, you all can get married in the rectory." So we were married in the priest's rectory. This was in 1945. We were supposed to get married July 12, but the lady hadn't finished my dress, so we got married Friday, July 13, 1945. The marriage lasted forty-one years, until Bob passed in 1986.

Selma Mackel Harris

I was born and raised in Natchez, Mississippi. My mother, Lucille Mackel, is a Catholic, and I was christened Catholic in New Orleans, so, when I became of age, I received communion here at Holy Family, and that's as far as I go, that far back.

Charles Harris, Jr.

I was christened in the church as a baby just like most babies. And I've grown up from a baby through adulthood in the Catholic Church. My parents are converts, but all of their children were baptized as babies, so we grew up in the church, and we also went all the way through Catholic school. Then I married a Catholic.

Charles Harris, Sr.

Now my mother and father was Baptist. I got married in 1930, and my wife had become Catholic by taking instruction. She would always try to get me to join the Catholic Church, and I told her I never would join it. I'd say, "My mother and father was Baptist." But she kept after me; she'd say, "Just go in and talk to Father Flanagan." So I talked to Father Flanagan. I think he was about seventy years old then, and he talked so good. He said, "I'm not going to tell you to join the church. Just read this and make up your mind. If you want to join, come back, and I'll give you instruction."

So I started reading the catechism and taking instructions. Then another friend of mine named David Jenkins started taking instruction along with me. When we took our first holy communion, we didn't even know when to go take it. All the children were on the altar rail, and Father called out, "Charlie, David...." And he told a little boy, "Get over and make room for them." So we took our first holy communion; then he confirmed us.

Father Flanagan was really something. I was crazy about that man. On Christmas, he would start preaching, and the first thing he would say was, "I know everybody wants a white Christmas, but I want a green Christmas." He meant he wanted some dollars, you know. And every Christmas, he would tell people "Happy Easter" because there were some people he knew he wasn't going to see any more until Easter, and every Easter he'd tell them "Merry Christmas."

So that's how I become a Catholic. I never have forgotten him.

Ora Frazier

When we were married, you had to make the commitment that the children would all be Catholic. I made that commitment, even though I was not a Catholic at the time. So I would go to Mass with Frazier; then I'd go to the Baptist church and back and forth, back and forth. I really didn't like that setup, but I liked going to the Baptist church. Then, after my youngest child, my daughter, was born, I made a commitment, right there during labor, that I wanted my family to be together, and I would become Catholic.

People often think that you go to another church because you feel the church you're in is not the right place, but that was not my reason. My main reason was so that we would be together as a family, and I didn't think we could be a strong family with me going to one church and the children and their dad going to another. So after my daughter, Denise, was baptized, I said, well, I'm going to go on and take the instructions. And I did, mainly because of the family ties that I wanted. There some things I didn't understand about the Catholic Church, but after going through the instructions, I didn't see a whole lot of difference between the two because we were all serving the same God.

There was a little difference in communion. It was hard at first for me to see that we were actually receiving the body, but after studying and praying, I can understand that, too. I never had a problem with confession. My daddy used to tease me all the time, "Oh, you got to go in there and tell the priests all your problems, huh?" and I said, "Well, it's no different from telling a close friend of mine."

Sidney Gibson

At the school, we had catechism every morning. That didn't bother my parents. They knew that was part of the curriculum. They never complained about it, and they never said, "I don't want you to become a Catholic." So we more or less grew into it. I didn't actually become a Catholic until I was out of school. I was in the service in Oklahoma when I was baptized. I had practiced as a Catholic for, I guess, twelve or thirteen years and went in the service, and got baptized after I was in the service for about two months.

I came out of the service and was married in the church, and my children were raised in the church. My wife is Baptist, and we were actually married twice. We were married in the Baptist Church, and then again in the Catholic Church. There wasn't any conflict or anything. It was just something that we wanted to do, and we did it. And we never have any problems between her church and mine. We get along fine. She attends her church, and my kids and myself attend Holy Family. On special occasions, she goes to church with us, and, occasionally, I'll visit her church.

We're going into fifty years of marriage now. We haven't been separated during the fifty years we've been together, and we haven't had any conflict that amounted to anything. We've been getting along fine.

Willie Dorsey Parker

My grandmother was a Catholic, Bessie Remus Dorsey. Back in the 1920s, the high water brought her and her sister over from Louisiana. From my understanding, some white people raised them and made them be devout Catholics. That was my grandmother Bessie Remus Dorsey and Lettie Lewis's mother, Fannie Hall. We all were baptized as infants at Holy Family.

My grandmother finished raising me after my mother died in the Rhythm Nightclub fire. The majority of my family died in that fire, April 23, 1940. My mother, two aunts, one uncle, Warren, and Lettie Lewis's brother Richard Hall all died. So, my grandmother finished raising us.

My grandmother was an intelligent person. She was a schoolteacher, and she was a beautiful person, save for the Lenten season. Then she would have us strung out every morning going to Mass, whatever the weather. We'd walk to Mass, go home, and come back for school, and at night, back to Mass. And everyone had to have a rosary in his hand. You recited on your way to church, and if you skipped a bead, she would look and see who missed the bead. Very strict she was.

When I was growing up, I felt like the kids who went to Broomfield School [the black public school] snubbed us. It was just a division there. If you didn't see it, you could feel it. They thought we made ourselves more than them, being Catholic. But it wasn't like that; they didn't give us a chance to be close. Underneath it, they might think that being Catholic was a white person's religion. I heard that from people. "That's a white man's religion." But I say it's one God. Nobody knows his color. Surmise a guess. He's white, he's black, he's green, he's orange, he's yellow, whatever. There's one God, and that's what I go on.

Some people had the feeling that we black Catholics shouldn't have happened, but I cannot go back and change history. This is all I know, to be a Catholic, a black Catholic.

On the job where I work, I'm the only Catholic, black or white, but it doesn't bother me. Just as they say, "I'm proud to be American"—well, I'm proud to be Catholic. I'm proud that I know Christ. I was raised in his book, and he puts his arm around me. He rocks me. This is all I know.

Chapter 7

A Place to Turn

Lavera Gibson Allen

Holy Family has always been viewed by the community as a haven for peace—somewhere they could always go. The church door was always open. You could walk in at any time. The Father and Sisters were always people that you could turn to for help. We used to have more Sisters than we have now, so it was easy to reach someone, and I think that's what the community liked.

Margie Hoggatt

The Sisters just mean everything to me. I don't know how I would have raised my children without their help. They have been good to me down through the years. They paid my rent, and told me don't say nothing about it. My husband didn't have work, and they bought me groceries and said don't tell nobody. And, when I first got my job at Jeff Davis Hospital, Sister Francis took me to the hospital.

Sister Francis was actually a Sister at Cathedral. I met her in the alley out there where I live. It was nothing but the Lord. I was standing on the porch; the rent lady had told me to move, and I didn't have anywhere to go or any money to move with. And Sister Francis come up; I was standing in the door. I said, "Hey, Sister." And she said, "Hey." She was looking for another woman who did some work for them at their house. She went on, but on her way back, she stopped again. She come up on the porch and say, "How are things, Margie?"

I said, "Bad as they can be." Then, she said, "What's goin' on?" and I told her. I say, "I don't know what I'm going to do; I'm just worried to death." My husband wasn't working, and I was just working by the day for people. Wasn't getting but two dollars a day when I got it. And Sister Francis said, "I'll deal with you in the morning, early, about six-thirty. I'm going to carry you somewhere."

I said, "All right," and, sure enough, that next morning, she came. She told me, "I've got you a dress." I didn't have nothing hardly fitting to wear, and she brought me this two-piece, blue-and-white suit to wear, and we went to the hospital. Sister knew this lady there who was a supervisor. She talked to that lady about me and told her that from the looks of her house, I know she's a good housekeeper and everything, and she's smart, and she wants to work.

It happened that there was this girl who was going to take off for breast surgery, and I was just supposed to take her place temporarily. But she died. She didn't never come back to work, and after she died, I just got her job. Been at the hospital for thirty-three years now. Wasn't that something?

Eugene Dottery

Black people in Natchez always respected Holy Family Church. They didn't like true religion, but they appreciated what the church was doing. They really did. They wouldn't themselves want to become Catholic because they had them ideas about the idols and praying to the priests and stuff like that, but they realized that the church was doing a lot of good work for the community. So we always had the respect of the community.

Vernon Williams

Father Mulroney was pastor during the Rhythm Nightclub fire; he was just ripping and running all over the place down there trying to find his people during that fire. It was in 1940. The building and the club burned. Some of the people were burned so bad, they had to bury them right away. I know we didn't find my brother Johnnie until the next day; he was burned so bad. We found him down at this parlor. They had bodies stored all out in the back of that garage. They just laid body after body out there, and I finally found him there and recognized him, and I went to see if Father Mulroney was over at the hospital.

They was working him to death all morning at the Charity Hospital; they were just filled with people. There was 212 killed, so you can imagine how many were hurt. So that's where Father Mulroney was.

Mazie Belle Rolax

Everybody said, "Rhythm Nightclub is on fire." So people just started walking from all over town, trying to see who of their people were there—who was in it and who wasn't. Two of my classmates, the Alexander sisters, were in it. My godmother, Mildred Washington, was in it. My brother's girlfriend, Henrietta, was in the fire. We were so upset. My brother was supposed to go to the club, but he and Henrietta happened to be spatting a little bit, and he didn't go. But she still went with another fellow, and they were both burned up in the fire.

The Rhythm Nightclub was a big tin building so the water they used to put out the fire turned into steam. Those people were burned, and they were steamed and every other thing. There was only one little entrance at the front door of the nightclub, and the people all ran to the front. They were like cattle. The ceiling was decorated with Spanish moss, and all that moss caught fire and started falling on the people, too, which made it worse. One person got in the refrigerator and survived. It was a sad thing, the way some just burned, and some was almost charred. And people told me that some of the Baptists that went, the ministers didn't want anything to do with them, because, at that time, it was a sin for the Baptist people to dance.

Father Mulroney was the pastor at Holy Family then, and his assistant was Father Dougherty. And they were busy. They really worked. Father Dougherty was helping everybody. There were a good number of Catholics in the fire. And the Rhythm Nightclub was down St. Catherine's, only about a block from the church. I remember Father Dougherty was just walking over bodies and ran himself ragged.

That night we went to all the morgues. People was just stepping over bodies up there at Mackel's funeral home. The smell was horrible. They had people just lying on the floor. There were way over two hundred people who died from the fire. I think there must have been a hundred and something to die that night. Then people kept dropping off and dying for days. My classmate, Suzie Alexander, wasn't burned anywhere but her head. She may have smothered to death, and her hair was burned off. Henrietta had a place on her leg, and her hair was burned, but she looked all right otherwise.

They talked about that fire for years in Natchez, and they still have the shrine down on the bluff, by the river, and there's a memorial service every year. I guess it's down there, instead of at the actual location of the club, so everybody can see it. You know—white, black, or whatever.

Joe Frazier

I lost my mother and father in the Rhythm Nightclub fire, and the Red Cross came to my assistance. Frankly, Father Mulroney wrote a note for me. We went to the Red Cross, and we got help with food and things. There were a lot of people who did not, who were unable to get in the system, and so Father Mulroney went and got help for Catholics and non-Catholics alike. And I do know of a number of families that joined the Catholic Church because of the love and the help that was given by the priests during that terrible time in Natchez. One out of every three black families lost somebody in that fire. It wiped out our senior class. It wiped out a lot of young parents.

So, everybody, more or less, needed assistance in some kind of way, and not just spiritual assistance. A lot of people came to the Catholic Church. All were not baptized, but they came out of respect, and thankfulness for the way the Catholic nuns and priests went out to help the people. That's the kind of support and the kind of respect that the black community had for Holy Family and for the Catholic Church. During those times of need, the Catholic priests and the nuns and the people of the church went out of their way to help all people and not just Catholics. They made things happen, and that built up the respect and the prestige that people had for the Catholic Church.

Vernon Williams

Take Father Mulroney, or Father Betzenhauser; you couldn't go anywhere in this town—north, south, east, or west, that they wouldn't know and recognize. Father Gaudette was the same way, and he was a much younger man. He would go anyplace. Anywhere his people were, he'd go there. He'd go and get his boys playing hooky. He'd go in the poolroom and get them out of there and bring them back to school. The poolroom was on Pine Street, what they call Martin Luther King now. It was in a kind of rough section of town. I'd say, "You got a lot of nerve going in that poolroom." But he'd say, "Well, it doesn't bother me." He didn't mind doing it.

Wilbur Johnson

Back in the years when black teenagers had problems even being on the street, there was respect for kids from Holy Family because there was a priest by the name of Father Gaudette who took a tremendous effort to make sure that we were guaranteed some privileges. Generally, the police would harass you when you were on the street, saying, "Nigger, where you going? You better get your so-and-so off the street before I get back." But they would also always ask, "Where do you go to school?" Because they knew that if we were from Holy Family, Father Gaudette would come around and have some input. He also had influential white friends in the community that would create some problems. So the police tried to avoid that as much as possible.

David Lewis

Holy Family played an important part for the African American people in Natchez, because there was a time that the police department was hard on black people. I'll give you an example that happened to me. I was seventeen. On Franklin Street, they had an ice cream parlor where all of us would hang out on Sunday. This policeman came down there and he was going to put three of us in jail. Said we was blocking the sidewalk.

So the squad car came around, siren going, and this policeman came out and said, "He's blocking the sidewalk." The other officer said, "You can't take these niggers on blocking no sidewalk 'cause all of them hang out here."

The first one said, "No, take them on." So they took us, and the desk sergeant said, "What you got these niggers for?" The policeman said, "They was around on Franklin Street and blocking the sidewalk."

The desk officer said, "Most of the business there is nothing but niggers, so why you going to lock them up?" He said, "I can't put them in jail."

Two of us were seventeen, and one was eighteen, but he didn't have his draft registration card, so they kept him until his brother went home and got his registration card, but they couldn't hold us. Then the same policeman, about a week later, came down, and I was standing up there, and he hit me across my chest with his billy club. Said, "I told you about standing around here." So I just walked off and went around on Main Street.

It was hard during that time. You couldn't hardly walk the street because the police would bother you. But every time they would arrest a Catholic, Father Gaudette would go around there, and he would raise Cain and get them out.

Father Gaudette did a lot for the kids in those days. He even had a youth center he opened up to keep us out of the poolroom. A place called the Ace Theatre had gone out of business, and he rented it and put three pool tables in there, and some more things for the kids to have somewhere to go.

Joe Frazier

I remember one occasion in particular; we had gone to play basketball down at Thibodeaux, Louisiana, and we didn't get back until, like 2:00 a.m. And the guy's mother who's supposed to pick us up, she got tired. So we had to end up walking, and, when we were walking, the police stopped us and said, "Come on, get in this car." They were fixing to put us in jail. "Where do you think you're going this time of night?"

We had the warm-up suits with the hoods on, and I guess we did look kind of intimidating, all of us coming down the street with hoods on our heads. That's probably the reason he stopped us.

We told them that we went to the Catholic school, and we had been playing basketball, and we were just getting home, and the person who was supposed to pick us up probably didn't know how late we were coming, so we had to walk home.

Believe me, at that time, policemen were to be feared. But they told us, "Well, look, you all be careful when you go. If anybody bothers you, you tell them we're watching you all on your way home."

At that time, we didn't look at the police as being friendly, but, when we told a policeman that we were just coming from Catholic school, they backed right off.

Elsie Jackson

Father Gaudette cared about black people. Not that the other priests weren't good, but back before civil rights and all of that, Father Gaudette was the man that took a stand for us. Whatever was going on, there was no closed doors to Holy Family members, no matter where.

They didn't like it, but Father was always with us, like going to the Eola Hotel and places like that. He would take members of the parish to the Eola to eat, back when everything was still segregated. The Eola was the fanciest place in town—strictly whites-only. But they were open for us because he was there with us, and no matter what, they respected that. They probably thought this man was crazy, so they paid no attention to him.

He would sing for those white people, too. He was a great singer. He'd sing at weddings and things, for money, and bring it on back to the church. And he'd always take a bunch of us along to hear him. This was back in the late 1940s, early '50s.

Chapter 8

New Day Coming

Louisa Quinn

I tell you, you wouldn't want to live here before they started the civil rights movement. There were just so many places that black people couldn't go—like cafés. So many places was off-limits to us. Even in the buses, you had a place where the blacks sit, behind a curtain or something, and the whites all sit to the front.

Edith Jackson

What brought on the civil rights movement was things like segregation, and the signs—black and white for everything. And we needed to get people hired in certain jobs, like the better-paying jobs. Another thing was that the police force didn't have blacks on it. Eating places had the whites on one side, and the blacks on the other. And we just thought that people had a right to sit wherever they want to.

We went marching to the courthouse because we felt that black people were paying taxes, and these things needed to be corrected. To do that, we had to vote. Every time we went to the courthouse, we had to fill out a questionnaire on the constitution. I think I did it about three times. Every time you did it, they'd say that you almost made it. Finally, they said that I had passed, and they wanted me to pay two dollars for poll tax.

Barbara Washington

I don't know why the Caucasians had the idea that they are supposed to be so superior over the blacks, or anybody else. I really can't get it in my mind why they would think they are better, or that God cares more for them than for us. From listening to them, you would think that we were monkeys, apes—anything but a human being. But I always thought that I was just as great, or maybe greater, than the next one. I've always known that I was a human being.

Reverend Shead Baldwin

I'm an outspoken fellow. What comes up, comes out— even on my job. And a lot of people hated that. I think that's where my work for civil rights originated; I was speaking out on the job at Armstrong Tire and Rubber. I first went to that job in 1946. I was about twenty-five years old, just out of the service. One of my first days there, I went to the cafeteria. When I found it, I just went on through the first door. When I went through that door, they told me, "You ain't supposed to come in here." I said, "Well, they told me at the office to come to the cafeteria."

They said, "You don't come in here. You get out."

I said, "Well, I'm not going out. I'm not going out till I get some explanation why."

They said, "The reason why is that you're black."

I said, "Well, that's not a reason for me to get out of here."

Finally, the manager came over and talked with me. He said, "You're right to go in. But suppose you go into this other door here?"

I said, "Why didn't they tell me about a special door when I went there? They told me to go through that door, and that's the door I went through, and now all of this other stuff started."

So one fellow, he told me, "You don't go out, I'll throw you out."

Now I was just out of the service, you know. So I said, "Well, I tell you, I've been in the Pacific, and I've been fighting. If you want to try and throw me, you come on." I knew a lot of judo at that time. But that is where they started picking at me, and that's how I got involved in all this.

I started at Armstrong mixing rubber for twenty-six cents an hour. It was a union plan—Rubber Workers Local 303. But back then the jobs were segregated pretty much by race. They had what you call white-collar jobs and black jobs. The company put an available job up on the board, and you'd sign for it by seniority. A lot of times if you would sign for a job, and you had the most seniority, they'd just go and erase your name off the board. You couldn't tell whether the company was doing it or whether some of the employees was doing it. But you knew one thing; your name wasn't up there.

There was a lot of stuff in that plant. We had a big water fountain where the whites drank and a little one where the blacks drank. So I was a union steward, and I went in one morning and a black fellow came to me and said, "I drank some water at that big fountain over there. The little one's broke."

I said, "Yeah."

He said, "They got me up to go to the office this morning."

I said, "Well, I'm going to move it to the next step. I got a union committee member I know, and I'm going to see what he has to say before you go in there."

So I went to this union guy, and I told him about the case. He said, "That fellow ain't nothing but a troublemaker. He knows he's not supposed to drink out of that fountain."

I said, "You supposed to be a workers' representative. You've got a bad attitude. The fountain broke, and the closest fountain is way across in another department. Was he supposed to leave out of his department when you got a rule against that?"

"Hell, no," the guy says, "but he is a troublemaker anyway."

I said, "Okay, since you got that attitude, you got two troublemakers. Put me in the case." Then, I went and got all them fellows and lined 'em up, and that's how we broke it up. After that, everybody drank out of the fountain. Then the white guys started putting their water in a container and bringing it in, so the company stopped that. The next thing that happened was we started going in the restrooms, when they still had the black and white restrooms. We started going in all the restrooms. So they wouldn't go in no restroom; they'd go outside. So the company says, "Anybody who goes outside stays outside."

So, we finally broke it up, but this was a real tough, tough thing back then.

Sidney Gibson

I worked in the factory for International Paper Company for twenty-three-and-a-half years. During the whole period that I was working at IP, before the civil rights movement, I was always active as a labor union representative. I was involved with fair employment practices and this kind of thing from the '50s on.

Around 1951, we organized a black local at the IP plant because we wasn't being properly represented by the white union officials. I was the president of that. It was called St. Catherine Local 747. We just came up with that name. I was kind of proud of it. We met in the Catholic hall just off St. Catherine Street. We talked with Father Gaudette, and we used the Catholic hall as a meeting place for more than fifteen years.

In 1954, we started to push for better jobs, more fair employment practices, and I went to the Southern AFL-CIO conventions in Mobile, Alabama, in '55, '56, and '58. I must have went about six years in all. I got a couple of people here together, and we drew up a fair employment practices resolution. We got it passed out of the resolutions committee because I had two white people who were pretty friendly to me, Claude Ramsey and W. A. Sims. Sims was from here; Ramsey was from down at Moss Point, Mississippi. They were on the AFL-CIO staff, and they were both on the resolutions committee. So we got the resolution out before the whole assembly.

It wasn't going to pass, because people were afraid of being fired, or worse. I was criticized by one of the international vice presidents. We had a lot of words back and forth, and then a minister from George County, South Carolina, came to my aid. He said it was a pity for men to be having those kind of words when we were all union people. Then he said, "I know we're not going to vote here for a fair employment resolution, but we could at least show the respect of being human, Christian people. We're acting like a bunch of devils." The preacher went on, "In fact, we all are a bunch of devils, including me. I'm not going to vote for it because I'm afraid."

Mamie Mazique

Marge Baroni was a very nice, married lady. She had three boys, I believe, and two girls. And her husband, Louis, was just so timid, you know. He worked at Armstrong Tire and Rubber Company. She came from right out here in Adams County, out in the country. She became a Catholic when she married Louis, and they belonged to St. Mary's Cathedral, the white Catholic church.

Marge was a nice looking lady, you know. She wore all kinds of haircuts—and was very frisky. She had a lot of energy. She loved to read and write, and she grew from that. She was a smart woman, really. She helped to open up a lot of avenues in the state of Mississippi, but especially in these three counties here—Adams, Jefferson, and Claiborne. She worked with everybody. She helped to plan and put things together and wrote proposals and organized.

All the time they was tearing up everything down here—demonstrating and picketing and marching and burning—she would go right in the middle of it. She would go to jail. I remember once they put my nephew in jail, and she said, "If you don't let him go, I'm going to jail, too." Her husband didn't want her to go to jail, but she said, "If Claude goes to jail, I'm going to jail." They couldn't make her come out of there. She went to jail for three or four days, and the only thing she would let them give her was a pillow and a book, and she stayed there; she stayed right there.

There was so much injustice, and you just had to stand up to them, you know.

Marge Baroni

After the Brown decision in 1954, and then when Dr. King began to get prominent with the Montgomery boycott, naturally everybody was beginning to discuss race more openly than in the past. I had children in school at Cathedral during those years, but they wouldn't discuss it over at Cathedral. Up until 1960, they would not teach the students the church's position on race. The children never heard it mentioned.

I'd talk about the race issue with my family and friends. They used to listen to me, and we used to discuss stuff that was academic—up until the time of the school desegregation in Little Rock in 1958. Before that, it was perfectly acceptable for white people to sit down and talk about how black people were mistreated, so long as one didn't do anything about it. You could deplore it. You could be upset about it. You could say it was wrong. You could read the Bible, and you could study your religion, but you couldn't practice it.

So I stopped going out at all, because every entertainment here was segregated. I belonged to the Community Concerts Association, and I worked for the local newspaper. I did reviews and things of that kind and was editor of the women's page. I got around a lot. But it became impossible for me to go to plays and concerts and things like that because they were absolutely segregated.

I think the breaking point came at a concert at the Natchez High School Auditorium when a parishioner from

Holy Family tiptoed down the aisle and got the white priest to go out on a sick call. It just killed me. It was so totally wrong. So I stopped going to those things. If everybody couldn't go, then I wasn't going.

So our social life sort of dwindled. I remember we went to a party and our oldest son's basketball coach was there, and he kept baiting me about race. This coach was even the godfather of one of our children, a close friend. But he kept on saying that blacks were inferior, and I told him I tried to approach it on a scientific level.

This definitely was in 1955, because I remember I was reading Dorothy Day's autobiography, *The Long Loneliness,* at the time. I had become very aware of the gap between the teaching and the practice of the church with reference to race. I was giving this guy answers about race that I had gotten from Father Kenneth Harris, who had instructed me for my conversion to Catholicism. This man later dropped us as friends after I became publicly active.

That was probably the hardest thing I had to face—that the people teaching my children, and the nuns and priests, too, were like that. Not as stupid as that man, but their thing was prudence, you know. God's going to take care of it. Louis and I had discussed this kind of thing time after time. The newspapers, the government, the schools, all of the institutions had failed. Everything was geared to a racist, repressive society. So we knew that we had to teach our children ourselves. Because we couldn't let them grow up afraid to be friends with somebody because they were different. And it kind of put you out in left field; it kind of put you out there by yourself.

The Holy Family community—up to this time, I didn't really realize that it was there. I had been there a couple of times, but it never occurred to me that there was a whole other life in Natchez, in the Catholic church, that was going on. To me, the Catholic church was that church up there, where the white people went. And when I became aware of it, I began to sort of keep my eyes and ears open, because I felt that a ministry that was working with the poor, specifically the blacks, in the South, must be more attuned to social issues.

Then I met Father William Danahy, a Josephite. He was making some calls in the hospital, and I was there. And when I met him he said something that was a quote from [*Catholic Worker* co-founder] Peter Maurin. And I felt that anybody who knew who Peter Maurin was must be somebody I needed to know, and so I started cultivating his acquaintance. Father Danahy was just a twin spirit. He was somebody that I really needed, because he felt the racial injustices as I did, and he knew about them. He knew more specifically what surrounded every murder of a black person. He told me one time that Natchez had a smell of evil to it, even before the paper mill came here.

One of the things everybody knew about was the mistreatment of black prisoners by the police. A person that I had gone to school with, her husband ran a grocery store, and he had a pregnant black woman picked up by the police for shoplifting. He went down to the station, stood by and watched them beat the woman. She wouldn't confess that she had been stealing from him, so they tied her and beat her. Now, the store owner's wife told me this, and she was horrified, but there wasn't anything that she cared to do about it.

And these kinds of things just kept going on. There was no effort to hide the fact that blacks were treated worse than animals. Mississippi, in those days, was like a concentration camp. It was just that oppressive. We had all this beautiful land, and all these crippled people.

So the first thing that Father Danahy and I worked on together was when a woman had been shot up by a white man several blocks below Holy Family Church, out on East Franklin. The black community knew what happened. And so did some elements of the white community. The police knew and so did friends of the white man who had shot the woman. I think she had been his mistress for some time, and then she dropped him, or something like that. The newspaper had a front page story about this woman being shot, and nothing was ever done about it. The news disappeared the next day.

I went down to the mayor of Natchez, Trayer Watkins. Off the record, he was quite willing to talk about the whole thing. He told me that they knew who had killed the woman, but they could never get an indictment. I asked him why. I said, "You know, we really need to have a discussion between the races in Natchez. We need to have a group to get together regularly, because we are going to have a lot of trouble."

He said, "Well, who's going to do it?"

And I said, "You are. You're the mayor of the town."

He said, "No, that would be the kiss of death, political suicide."

So I said, "Well, I'll do it."

He said, "You'll be ostracized." And I did, and I was.

I told Father Danahy what Mayor Watkins had said: that there was nothing we could do to get any prosecution, and there was no point in making an effort at interracial dialogue. So Father Danahy said that we would do it, and we would start off with women. There were two other white women that I knew at the time. Mary Grover was one. Both of them were Catholics, one a convert, and one a former nun, a Daughter of Charity. Father Danahy got three black women, and the six of us met over at Holy Family rectory. This was still back in the 1950s and nobody really knew what we were doing. We met for about a year. I know I had another baby during the process. We never really did anything, except talk about local problems. But we got to know each other on an equal basis, and we kept those relationships going. I've since realized why Father Danahy wanted to start out with women. The men would probably have been killed.

Joe Hall

Joe Frazier and I did a lot of things together in the Catholic community, mingling with the white church. There was this National Council of Catholic Men, whom the people around here dubbed Communists. It was a group all over the nation who got together to fight injustice in the United States and any other thing, I guess, pertaining to the church. The things that we dealt with were racial prejudice and discrimination.

There was a man that really tried to get the people of Cathedral parish together. It was a man by the name of Lester Mean. He ran a little sawmill or something out here. I don't know whether he was a rich man, but I guess he was well-off. We used to go out and meet with him and talk with him at his office. I remember once we were supposed to have a meeting up at Cathedral, and we were supposed to meet with him the night before at his office. We went out there, and when we walked in we could tell there was something wrong from the look on his face. We got to talking, and then he started getting these phone calls, and, after a while, he told us what it was. He was getting threatening calls, and people calling the National Council of Catholic Men nothing but a bunch of Communists. These were some of the good Catholic people, too.

We had one meeting. There was twelve or fifteen white men; Joe and I were the only blacks. We had a bunch of books and had subjects that we discussed. One of the volumes was *Discrimination and the Christian Conscience*. I remember that one.

After it got out that we had this thing, a lot of people were offended that these white men had been locked up with some blacks. Then they found out what we were talking about, and I think that Lester Mean started to getting a little hate, and he had to back off. And then it wasn't long before he took sick. He had a stroke. I don't think he ever recovered.

Chapter 9

Walking the Walk

Reverend Shead Baldwin

In September 1963, I had a church get burned down. I started rebuilding that church in July 1964, and then I had another church where I preached get burned down. Along that time, George Metcalfe, who was president of the local NAACP, came to me, and he said, "Well, we going to get organized to combat some of the problems here." At the time they were also calling our people out, especially an under-taker named Archie Curtis. The Klansmen called him out like somebody was sick, and he went out, and they got him and beat him up. We didn't start any action about that. Later on, they got two more fellows; one of them was a butler at Kingston mansion. They took him out and beat him up.

We decided to start taking action. So we went to Nosser's grocery store to try and integrate it. George Nosser was the mayor of Natchez at that time.

A little bit later, they bombed George Metcalfe and tried to kill him. When that happened, we started to get organized. We gave several demands to our city fathers. They had to do with getting black police on the police force, getting other black people working in the stores, and so on. We told them if they didn't do it, we was going to start marching and picketing and what-not. This was in the last of 1964. They said they would give us an answer at a later date, and, about three days later, they got 650 National Guard members brought in. We decided that we wouldn't do anything to cause bloodshed. We waited until the National Guard was gone and then we started to march. When we first marched, it was peaceful. The next time, the city put an injunction on us to keep us from marching.

We told them that we had constitutional rights, and this was a violation of our rights. But they said if anyone is out there marching, they're going to get arrested. So we just told them to get the jail ready because we're going to be there, and that's what happened. We went out to march, and they arrested a bunch of people. They filled up the jail; they didn't have anywhere to put them. They came and said to us, "Don't do it again." But we did, and they put them down in the City Auditorium. We had a bunch in there—several hundred people. They decided to send them to Parchman penitentiary. The Mississippi law says you're not supposed to send anybody to Parchman unless you have a legal court hearing, and the person is found guilty. So they violated that law.

Following that, we started going to the Armstrong Tire and Rubber Company about upgrading jobs for black people, and finally they asked Wharlest Jackson to work over one evening. He was our NAACP treasurer. He was working the dayshift at Armstrong, and they asked him to work over. He did, and that night, about 8:20, while he was driving home, a bomb went off and blew him clean through his truck cab. He was killed dead, on the spot.

They never did catch anybody for that. They knew who did it. The chief of police told me, "He's under surveillance. We're going to follow him." But they never arrested him.

From the time they killed Wharlest Jackson, we just kept moving.

We started a voters' registration drive. When we started, we had about 700 black people registered to vote in this county, Adams, and we registered something like 7,700 in our first drive. Second drive, we wound up with about 10,000 black people on the voters' roll. In Claiborne County, we had zero registered to vote, no black registered voters at all. So we put a team out there, and they got every person they could to register. In Jefferson County, it was zero, no registered voters there. We put a team in and got something like 2,800. Then, we went on to Wilkerson County where we had zero, and we got from 2,800 to 3,300 people registered down there.

So this is how our movement worked. We worked under the law. The Supreme Court or Congress would pass a law; we would work on it. We would work on it immediately, and we were fortunate enough to get people registered to vote, and to get people on different jobs. And we were fortunate enough to get some respect, other than just being called boy or girl or nigger. We wanted it to be just Mr. and Mrs. and that's the way we address everybody now, whether you're black or white.

This thing worked out pretty good.

Lucille Royal Mackel

My husband, Bob, had an uncle named Dr. Mackel; he was the first one that became involved in the movement, and he was harassed so much he moved to Chicago. After he moved, Bob and his brother, Walter, got really involved in it. They used to meet on St. Catherine Street. It was a frightening feeling, but when you went to those meetings the people from New York would come and tell you you're not supposed to be afraid. Looked like they would convert you not to feel fearful anymore. It was like a revelation.

So we were really and truly involved with the civil rights movement. A lot of the white girls from New York came and stayed here with me because my girls were off in college. That's when we were trying to register people to vote.

That was really something. Sometimes you'd go to the courthouse, to the clerk's office, and wait in line and get right there to the window, and they'd say, "We closed now. You have to come back tomorrow." They were trying to discourage you from learning how to vote.

I went up there myself to register, and it was just nerve-racking really. You just can't imagine human beings treating you that way. And a lot of us had been in these people's houses and helped raise their kids up, cooked their food, cleaned their houses. Why did they hate us so? We hadn't done them anything. Why were they like that?

But I'd just say, "Well, don't get discouraged. We'll be back tomorrow."

Charles Harris and Selma Mackel Harris

Selma: My dad was Robert Mackel, and he and his brothers were in a lot of the boycotts, the walks and all. And we were involved in quite a bit, too; we attended a lot of the mass meetings. There was a store across the street from our house, a supermarket that was being boycotted. We had a lot of people who stayed with us that came in from Montgomery and different places to help with the movement. A lot of them did some of the boycotting, you know, the walks in front of the store across the street. There was a lot of vio-lence—white people passing by with dogs, and the dogs jumping at the crowd, even gunfire in that area. It was really scary for us as young people. We were in it, but we were scared to death. Daddy tried to keep us away from it as much as he could, and he did what he could with his brothers.

Charles: Yeah, just being a youth at the time was exciting, in a sense, but it was historical, too, because black people were really together, and they knew what they wanted, and they were ready to fight and do whatever was necessary to get their freedom. You may find it hard to believe, but, dur-ing that time, in order to vote, you had to interpret the Constitution, and they could decide whether you interpreted it right or not. A lot of people were being discouraged not to vote. But we were persistent.

Julia Davis

I participated in the movement by being there when they had meetings. Anything that they did, boycotting and whatever, I was there. I marched. I got hurt one time when a carload of white men passed us. We had been marching to the courthouse that night. We had marched downtown from this church up here on Pine Street across from Cathedral. Can't remember which church it was; I can't remember all those Baptist churches. But, anyway, we had marched from this church to the courthouse, and we were on our way back, coming up Franklin Street, and this car just missed me. If this man hadn't pushed me back, they would've hit me with that car. We had, I think they called them godfathers, in that group that would protect the marchers and keep anything from happening to them.

The Ku Klux Klan was real bad here in Natchez. It was to a point that even the Baptist ministers were afraid to open their churches to the NAACP. That was the civil rights group here in Mississippi, which Charles Evers headed for the whole state after his brother, Medgar, was assassinated. Eventually they put the NAACP office in Holy Family Church.

We were boycotting the stores. They had a Black Christmas where we had boycotted those stores so that they had to close. Whether people believed in the boycott or they didn't, they was afraid to go in those stores. I remember going to Vicksburg and shopping for the children for Christmas. We went over to Louisiana, and we would shop for the children, but we wouldn't buy anything here in Natchez.

We had a grocery store right here, Lewis's, that went out of business. The boycott was very strong, and it helped a lot. A lot of people said that it wouldn't help. "You could boycott all you want; it wouldn't stop a thing!" But it did stop it. It definitely did. I remember walking this corner up here picketing. I would walk for, like, four hours.

Some of the merchants would come out and try to attack the walkers. We didn't go into their stores. We just had our signs. We would walk up and down that street, that sidewalk. And a lot of people stopped trading with them. Especially with the ones that really acted up toward black people; they stopped trading with them, period. You couldn't pay anyone to go in a store. Even the whites wouldn't go in and trade with them. Some of them felt the same way we did, but they were afraid to say anything.

I was blessed to be there for this part of my life. I really was; I'm glad I was there, so my children, and people that's coming along now, can get better jobs.

Sidney Gibson

We always put a lot of emphasis on nonviolent action. I figured people was more inclined to participate with nonviolence. Some people were a little more radical than we were, and we would never tell them they were wrong. We would just tell them we have our program, and you have yours. The majority of the people supported the nonviolent movement. It worked good. Our first boycott might be the most effective boycott in the history of the United States. It was really successful. It really set the stage for some forward movement. The boycott began to open things up, make people start to think.

It was targeted at stores, and we wanted the elimination of separate facilities. We wanted all public officials to use courtesy titles with people. We wanted the stores to begin to open their better jobs to black people. We had a lot of black women then working in stores here as maids. We wanted to move those people up to clerks or cashiers.

The boycott lasted about seven months, and we got the majority of our demands. We got written commitments from just about everybody: all the city and county officials and the majority of merchants and the merchant's association.

Also back then, we had a lot of students come down for the voter registration effort. They worked Amite County, Jefferson County, Claiborne County, Adams County, Franklin County. We had them from all over, from just about every college in the country. Everybody participated, and everybody cooperated with getting the students placed in homes and things like that, lodging them and supporting them while they were here.

That's where Holy Family Church played a bigger role than most of the community was in housing the kids. They did a tremendous thing there, because a good bit of the kids that came in were Catholic kids—black and white. That's where our church played a bigger role than anybody else, furnishing housing, food, and transportation for the student volunteers.

Joe Hall

Later on Joe Frazier and I were called up to Jackson. They had one of those Catholic men's groups up there that was going through one of these retreats. They were coming to this session on discrimination and the Christian conscience, and they said to themselves this is ridiculous for us, a bunch of white men, to sit up here and talk about this. We need to have some other views, so they called and asked us if we would come, and a couple of black guys from Jackson came also.

While we were in Jackson, there was a riot here in Natchez. When we got ready to leave Jackson, I remember Joe saying, "Man, they got highway patrol at every exit from Natchez, and they are searching all the cars." He knew I carried a pistol all the time. Back then, even traveling the highway, you never knew when you was going to get stopped or bothered by somebody. I loved the ground that Martin Luther King walked on—and I got to admit that he was right in his nonviolence, but I never did espouse that, even when I marched here in Natchez. In a lot of towns there would be these white guys that were brave and ran up in the crowd and jumped on somebody, and I was glad that never happened here, because I wasn't going to follow that philosophy.

So Joe told me not to bring the pistol back from Jackson because they was going to search us. I said, "Okay. I won't." But I did anyway, and they didn't search us.

Now nonviolence was talked about at all the meetings and things. When they went out to march, they didn't expect any violence. But here in Natchez, we also had a group called the Deacons for Defense. They guarded around the meeting places, and they were nonviolent. As far as I know, they never had to do anything. They probably scared a few people off. But they were there. The people going to the meetings wouldn't see them, but they were there.

Robert Plummer

It was sometime during the 1960s, I think. I was in the tenth grade then, and Father Doyle was the pastor here at that time. There was a statue of Jesus in front of the church, and we always said, you know, Jesus was more of a dark colored race, and the statue had his face white. So me and some of the guys said, "Hey, let's paint it!" And we talked about it and talked about it for days, and we went to Father Doyle, and we mentioned it to him. We said that's what we're planning on doing; we're going to paint the statue black. And Father Doyle's remark was, "Well, Jesus was of a dark skin race." He made no other comment on it. But we was letting him know something. We wanted to show him that, "Hey, we believe in this religion, but the wrong color is on this statue out in front of the church, and this is a black parish, too." But we never did get to paint that statue; we never did do it.

Lettie Lewis

Now, you want to hear the truth, as far as the civil rights movement was concerned? I didn't know nothing about it. I heard and saw on television what was happening, but I'm not going to be in any kind of pushing and shoving and parading up and down the street; I never was.

But my youngest daughter, Jessica, was out visiting some friends on St. Catherine Street once, when they were having a rally at a Baptist church there, and my sister called me from Chicago. She said, "You got your TV on?" I don't remember what I told her, but she said, "Well, turn it on, honey, and look on there. You'll see your daughter on St. Catherine Street in the crowd going up in that church." And I had no idea she was even there. I thought she was at a friend's house, visiting some classmates. And there she was pushing and shoving in the crowd getting up in the church.

Chapter 10

Paying the Price

George and Louisa Quinn

Louisa: We had a man got bombed one night—Wharlest Jackson. They bombed him up, and we marched that night. Our pastor, Father Morrissey, prayed half the night right out there on the street where he got bombed. Wharlest Jackson was killed when the bomb went off in his truck. He was an official in the local NAACP, and he worked at the Armstrong tire plant. He had a position the whites didn't want him to have, and they bombed him up.

George: I was working at the Armstrong tire plant then. They bombed Wharlest Jackson because, at Armstrong Tire and Rubber, they had a paint house, where they mix up all these different paints, and he was running it. It was a high-paying job, and they didn't want him to have it.

Edith Jackson

I think it was 1965; it was on a Saturday. This particular march, organized by Charles Evers, came after several of our men had been bombed. What happened on this Saturday was a group of us was marching and came on the sidewalk, and one of the sheriff's personnel stated that if we grouped in twos, they was going to take us to jail. We decided to stay there, and they did take us—everybody there—in the bus, to the City Auditorium.

We stayed there until around 6:00 or 6:30 p.m. Then they made the statement that they was taking everybody to Parchman. They had the buses outside and lined everybody up. It was the sheriff's department carrying us to Parchman, so we didn't stop at any lights or anything, just carried everybody straight through.

When we got there, the personnel at Parchman came out with guns. Soon as the men got off the bus, they beat them a little bit with the butt of the guns. They stated that everybody was going to different cells. If you had a coat or whatever, you had to take that off, take your shoes off and put them in a pile. After that, they decided to give everybody a cup of some type of medicine. It was a laxative-type thing, chocolate, so we questioned whether we had to drink this. We would say, "No, we wasn't going to drink it." And they'd say, "Oh, yes, you are going to drink this."

I was in a cell with nine people. Every cell was given maybe one or two rolls of toilet tissue. That commode there was a terrible thing. It was a basin, or whatever it is, on the wall, and there wasn't any privacy for anybody. Whatever you had to do, everybody's there.

A lot of things went on in Parchman that people outside really wouldn't believe. The men were on the backside of us, and I understand they stripped the men, and they turned the fans on them. We could hear the noise. They were singing to keep warm. We didn't suffer as much; we did have our clothing on, but the men didn't have anything on. The food that they served you was terrible. I didn't eat, and a lot of other people couldn't eat because you could see the worms in the rice. The women needed personal things; some of them required sanitary napkins, but they wouldn't give them to us. We had one young lady who was pregnant, and they put her in a cell.

It was on a Saturday that our group went to Parchman, and I stayed there until Monday evening. That's when my family came and got me. Once we got out, I went to the church and met J. T. Robinson, a policeman, and I explained that he needed to get this young woman out because she had started spotting, and they probably had something on their hands with that. So I think that first thing the next morning, they did bring her back to the hospital, and the baby was born after that.

Barbara Washington

My oldest son, Glen Allen Davis, was a determined child. He attended all the civil rights meetings with his friends, the Logan children. They were determined to try to make things better. They marched, and they put them in jail, and I would have to go down and get him out. He was fifteen years old at that time. One Saturday morning they marched from Beulah Baptist Church up here on B Street, and they went to jail—my husband, Richard, too. He went to see about the boys. He and some of the men was standing on this side by Cathedral High School, and he just stepped off the curb to say, "Well, let me go in and see what the boys are doing," talking about his sons, and the police arrested him, took him to jail.

One of the other men came and brought me the keys to our car and told me, "Richard says you should come downtown and bring the car home." Now he and my son had told me that if anything happens, don't you come running around to the jail crying and getting us out right away. So I said, "Okay." When they went to jail, it was the early part of the afternoon, like one or two o'clock, and I didn't go to get them out right away.

Mamie Lee Mazique called and told me that they was getting ready to take them to Parchman and for me to go and get them, so I did, and the minute my husband walked up, he asked me, "What took you so long?"

I said, "You told me don't come and get you."

But he said, "You don't know what it was like."

They had the young people at the City Auditorium, so we went and got Glen.

The next day, Sunday morning, we were getting ready to go to church and Glen was putting on blue jeans and rough clothes. I said, "Glen, darling, is this what you're going to wear to church this morning?"

He said, "No, Mama, I'm going to march this morning."

I started crying, and I asked him, "Glen, please don't get in any marches. You're going to drive me crazy."

And he said, "Mama, I'm going to march." So he did.

That Saturday, they took a lot of them to Parchman and did them real bad. And that Sunday morning, Glen was with the first group that got on the first bus, and the next thing I knew, they were in Parchman, too. I talked to several people around here, Mamie Lee especially, and that Tuesday a group of folks got together and went to Parchman to bring them home.

When Glen came home, we had to put him in the hospital. He had pneumonia. They had stripped them of their clothes and turned water hoses on them, just all kinds of bad things, and he stayed down at General Hospital for about a week with pneumonia. He told about the ugly words they would say to him. And they gave them some kind of medicine to make them go to the bathroom—just all kind of bad things.

I really don't want to talk about it; I'll start crying. But it showed them that these younger black folks was not going to take what we took.

Lucille Royal Mackel

They had a lot of death threats on us, when my husband, Bob, was so involved in the civil rights movement. They always were accusing him and his brother, Walter, of a lot of things that weren't true. We used to let the kids that were marching come to our house and rest. We'd have sandwiches for them; they would go to our bathroom and stuff like that.

And I think because we did that, they were always saying that we were doing bad things. Like when the Nosser grocery store burned down. Somebody put gasoline on it, and it burned down one night. The Nosser store was right across the street from our house, and the movement was trying to integrate the store. So the FBI came and questioned Bob and Walter and said they were involved in the fire. Come to find out, after they investigated it, that the store owners had done this themselves to get the insurance money because they didn't want to integrate the store.

I think all the people who were so involved in the movement, it took a toll on their lives; it really did. Our pastor, Father Morrissey, after everything got settled, got real sick. My husband had a heart attack, and a lot of people got really sick after all this tension, you know. Bob kept a lot from us at the time—a lot of the threats. After the children grew up and got old enough to understand, my husband would sit down and tell us about the close calls that they had, and it looked like your hair would just rise on your head. I'd say, "Oh, my God, that happened and I didn't know anything about it?" I would really be frightened for him.

Like, one time this guy, Archie Curtis, who owned a funeral home, got called out on a rural road—Palestine Road. In those times, the people who ran funeral homes made the ambulance calls. If someone got violently sick, the hearse would go out like an ambulance and pick them up. These people called Archie Curtis out for some sick person. And, when they got him out there, they said that he was one of these smart niggers, so they were going to teach him a lesson. They whipped him and whipped him, just unmerciful, and they stripped him of his clothes and everything. Afterward, he got to a lady's house named Ms. Bell, and she called Archie's wife, Mary. When she got him home, she put him in a tub of warm water, and he was beaten so severely the water was just red. Soon after that, Archie Curtis had a stroke, but he lived quite a while after that beating. After that happened, whenever Bob or his brothers would go out on an ambulance trip, they would always have people in the back of the hearse with guns and stuff like that to protect themselves because they would get so many calls that really weren't sick calls.

Charles Posey

For a while, during the civil rights movement, we had Father Norville here at Holy Family. He was a black priest from Pascagoula, Mississippi. They had to get him out of

town. He was an outspoken priest for the civil rights movement and with that rectory being right there on the corner,
they could easily come by and throw a firebomb up there and
get rid of him. So they got him out of town; I don't know
where. I think he went to Baltimore.

Joe Hall

Holy Family Church was not involved in the movement
as a group, but a lot of people did what they thought was a
help on their own. I took part in a good many things, you
know. I went to the meetings; I went to the churches. Along
with Father Morrissey, I was in this Freedom Democratic
thing, you know, in 1964 when we challenged the National
Democratic Party. I went out to a few counties for meetings.
I'll never forget we went out to Amite County one night, and
that was the first time I had been away from Natchez for
anything, you know.

I knew all the policemen by faces here in Natchez. If we
marched, and they were on the streets, the heck with them,
they were on the streets. But, that night in Amite County, I
didn't know what to expect. I really don't know to this day
whether they intended to use the courthouse for this meeting,
or whether they just intended to get some media coverage
and challenge the local law. But, man, a big, old, white
policeman was up there on that courthouse lawn with them
dogs. And he told us, "You ain't coming up here, boys."

So our leaders argued with them a little bit, and they
finally went on to the place where they could have the meeting. But you never knew whether they was going to bomb
the place or not. I guess nobody would have gotten anything
done if they had worried about things like that. If you'd

worried about whether you were going to be killed going or coming, then you wouldn't go.

Louis Baroni

My wife Marge and I were ostracized in those years. I was ostracized at the Armstrong plant, except for a couple or three people. Marge was spat on by my neighbor right down the street, and people just didn't know what to think because we were different—my wife was different, mainly.

I wasn't involved as much as she was. But I was still ostracized because of what she did. I was in the Knights of Columbus at one time, and, during this period I was ostracized by the people in the Knights of Columbus. I grew up with these people, went to school with them—and I would be going in the church, and they would be right beside me, and they wouldn't speak. They'd just pretend they didn't see me. I thought that was a little bit hypocritical to be a member of the Knights of Columbus and ostracize your fellowman.

At one point, the FBI moved into some apartments across the street from our house. They called us one day and said they wanted to come over and talk to us, and we said they could. We wanted to know why they were over there, and they said, "Well, we're over there to protect your property."

I said, "Protect my property? What about my life?"

And they said, "Well...." They didn't have much of an answer for that, so they advised me to leave my car at home when I went to work because it might be bombed. I did that for about six months, and the more I thought about it, the more I just wasn't going to live like that, so I began taking my car to work and parking it outside the plant, and nothing ever happened.

My wife was called a nigger-lover and all that kind of stuff. And, of course, the Klan knew about Marge, but she never worried about the Klan. They followed Marie Grover and Marge over to Holy Family one particular night, and, while they were in the building, the Klan just kept circling the block. When they got ready to leave, they saw them circling the block, but they didn't do anything.

My wife had courage. I didn't have the courage that she had. She knew that she could be riding down the street and be shot, but she never worried about that.

Marge Baroni

There were days and days back then, weeks and months even, that I couldn't go look at the Mississippi River, because so many bodies were being found there. When those three guys were murdered up in Neshoba County in 1964, the search for the bodies came all the way down to Natchez. They dragged the river right here, and they found bodies they didn't even know were missing. They found two Alcorn College students from Lorman, Mississippi. These two young people had been cut in half with a saw; mortar blocks tied to them, their hands were tied behind their backs. Pieces of their bodies were picked out of that river. We know who did it. Anyway, I just couldn't go to the river. We used to go and look at the sundown, but I had to quit going. I could not stand it.

After the Philadelphia killings in the summer of 1964, Bobby Kennedy appointed a special task force to investigate violence in the South. One day Father Morrissey was at my house, and the phone rang. It was my pastor at St. Mary's, Monsignor Fullem. He said that Father Law [later Cardinal Law] had called from Jackson and asked him to contact us and have us come to the rectory of St. Mary's Cathedral. We went up to the rectory and met these men. They were sent down here by the attorney general to do whatever they could to keep things cool. They had come to leave one of their number, a representative of the federal government, here in Natchez.

Of course in those days, every out-of-town car and every stranger in Natchez was noted by the police. It was their responsibility to report strangers and find out what they were doing. And so these two government men, knowing that, had parked their car four or five blocks away from Cathedral and walked back up. Also they wore ordinary clothes—polo shirts and things like that. But they parked in front of the post office and got spotted. We met them for about two hours, and Monsignor Fullem got nervous. He was always afraid Cathedral was going to get bombed, and he told them they had to leave. Their car had been down there for two hours, and he knew it had already been spotted, and they would just have to leave. He wanted the government men to go out the front door, Father Morrissey to stay in the house, and for me to go out the back door, through the sacristy, stay in the church and say three Hail Marys, and then go out the front door of the church to the hall. So I did that.

The government man who was going to stay in Natchez got scared and went back to Baton Rouge that night, but he did come back in a few days and did good work here. But even when they were here, they didn't stay on the weekends, which was when things happened. They would tell us to call anytime, call collect, but you couldn't do that. Especially since the telephone company had people in the Klan working for them. And the man who was sheriff at that time has since told us that he was informed every time somebody new registered in a motel.

When the Civil Rights Commission members would come down, I would meet them at the A&P to find out who they wanted to see, and I would lead them. If we had anything to say, we'd get out of our cars, and he would be getting something out of his trunk, and I would be putting something in my trunk. And I would tell him, in a very low voice, what I wanted to say. It was that kind of thing. It was a matter of life and death.

Finally, it was decided that the U.S. Commission on Civil Rights would hold a hearing—they called it the Mississippi Advisory Council. There were some brave people who served on the Mississippi Advisory Council—black men and black women, and white women, and two white ministers, and maybe a priest. But I don't think the priest was from Mississippi. And we had a public hearing in the basement of the post office building on Main Street. I went with two other white women. And we heard people tell about the total lack of protection. People in rural counties, as well as here in Adams County, were totally without protection of their lives. They were totally at the mercy of the terrorists. And at midpoint of that hearing, I heard Archie Curtis talk about having been taken out on a false alarm and horsewhipped by the Klan. Archie must have been about sixty-three at the time. He had a stroke; it was a really bad thing.

When I got home that night, I got a call. I had been talking all the time on the phone with the president of the local NAACP, George Metcalfe. It was supposed to be a secret, but I'd gotten his name from Mrs. Mazique and looked up the number. So George Metcalfe called that night and said he had seen me that day. I said, "Well, I wish you would have said something." And he said that he couldn't because the hearing had been invaded by the Klan. The way the Klansmen got our seats at the hearing was they had us informed that there was a bomb threat. We didn't take it seriously; we just moved back into another room in the same basement floor of the post office. After they had carefully searched to find out there was no bomb, we went back and there the Klansmen were sitting in our seats. They were there to intimidate the witnesses who were telling about the lack of law enforcement.

But George Metcalfe had seen me that day. We had just been voices on the telephone before then. So I said, "Well, maybe somehow I could see you." We kept on talking. He kept on calling me. By that time, he would be calling me to report things that had happened, so I could get news to the outside. So one day he called me and told me he had seen me again, when I was taking my children to school. I said, "Well, I just have to know who you are."

He said, "What time do you take the children to school?"

And I said, "Usually about 8:15."

He said, "I work from midnight to 8:00 a.m. I'll sit on the steps of the Union Hall, and I'll make you know me."

So the next day I drove in front of Armstrong Tire and Rubber, looking all around, with my eyes on the steps of the Union Hall, and this tall person stands up and nods. I looked, and I nodded. I didn't even turn my head. I just dipped my eyes and nodded to let him know that I had seen him, and I knew who he was.

Can you imagine being so scared to speak to another human being? Or to know who another human being is?

Some of my friends used to tell me not to be so angry. But I was angry as hell, and very bitter, because the ordinary, simple acts of human kindness were forbidden.

Sidney Gibson

I was threatened a lot on the job because of the things I was doing. I had a lot of threats, but most times you just didn't think about it. Sometimes you'd walk around the job and somebody knows where you're going, and they'll pin a note up on a locker where they know you was going to see it. But I never really paid a whole lot of attention to it. At one time, all of my insurance doubled because the insurance company considered me a bad risk. That's the explanation they gave me when I questioned it. "Well you're just a bad risk. You're involved in too many things, and too many people are threatening you."

For a while, in fact, for a good while, about six years, IP [International Paper] claimed they couldn't let me work on the night shift. They figured it was in my best interests—for my safety—so I just worked during the daytime.

I have done a lot of things that I guess a lot of people wouldn't dare do. I was having Klansmen subpoenaed before the House Un-American Activities Committee. I had a list of people who was actually Klan members and Klan sympathizers. I got copies of this, and they knew about it. I had folks subpoenaed from inside the IP mill by the Un-American Activities Committee because I was working with one of the FBI agents here.

Then they had the incident down here with Ben Chester White, an old man who got shot and killed down in Kingston. Ben Chester White was uninvolved in the movement. I think he went to church once in a while, but he didn't even go to any civil rights meetings. He was just an old man who sat around the grocery store down there. He'd go in and get a cake and a bottle of pop, and he'd sit there on a bench and talk to people going by. I couldn't ever understand why they would do that to him, until later I was talking to a man who said he was a former Klansman. He told me that Martin Luther King had been in Jackson, and they were trying to lure him in here to kill him. They killed old man White and figured Dr. King would just get excited and run on in here, and they could get rid of him.

Three of the people involved in killing Ben Chester White was working at IP. Avant, Fuller, and Jones—that was their names. They wasn't convicted for it in state court, but they convicted them in federal court. Then I filed charges against IP for letting them work, because IP has a rule that anybody who is convicted of a felony couldn't work at IP. So I had them fired.

People ask me if I was afraid during the civil rights movement. It's the truth, you do get scared, and a lot of times we marched at night. We were always near the front of the line, and we believed if someone was going to be shot with a high-powered rifle, it was going to be some of us. We knew this was a Klan stronghold, and we had decided that, even though we were afraid, it was something that was going to have to be done. Somebody was going to have to do it.

I told my wife, "Well, I've had a full life. I've done right things, and I'm proud of it; if this is the time it's going to happen, this is the time it's going to happen. Somebody's got to get out there and do it." That's what you do. We was some scared people. And we didn't deny it among one another; we discussed it. That's what gave us the courage to keep going.

Chapter 11

Father Morrissey

Jacob Larry

Father Morrissey was a character. He was a heavyset guy, Irish. He had an Irish accent, but he was from New York. He was in a seminary up there where he became a Josephite priest, and they just kept moving him around. All his relatives had died except for a cousin in Chicago that he called Jane.

Father Morrissey ate a lot. He drank a good deal, too. He drank a good deal of beer, and he had a big stomach. When his health kind of went bad, the doctor told him he couldn't have any more alcoholic beverage, period. Then he started drinking nonalcoholic beer. He passed at the age of sixty-five years.

He was really involved with all the civil rights movement. And he had a lot of big influence in Washington and New York. He was a man that could get things done. He had Robert Kennedy down here. Father Morrissey picked him up at the airport in Jackson, and carried him all the way up through Greenville, and showed him what kind of housing that the blacks was living in; the condition that things was in. The Catholic diocese started a big, low-income housing project up in Greenville that Father Morrissey helped spearhead.

When he left Holy Family, he went to Fayette, in the next county. The Josephites usually allow a priest to stay something like seven or eight years. Father Morrissey had been at Holy Family for eight years, from 1961 to 1969, so it was time for him to move. So, he just moved over from Natchez to Fayette. He became pastor of St. Anne's Parish in Fayette, which is a small church. The people up there didn't like it because Father integrated the church. They had a church in Harrison for the blacks, and then they had a church in Fayette for the whites. They was both Catholic churches. Father consolidated the two churches and put both of them in Fayette. That was in 1971. Most of the whites left and started going to church in Port Gibson. He stayed in Fayette for fifteen years and died there in 1984.

After moving to Fayette, Father Morrissey helped Charles Evers get elected mayor. He was the first black mayor in Mississippi since Reconstruction times. Then Charles Evers went on to try to run for governor, and Father Morrissey was involved in that. Then he got into politics himself and ran for the state senate. That was somewhere later in the 1970s. That got Bishop Brunini upset. The bishop didn't want the church into politics. He said he didn't want any of the churches in his district endorsing candidates.

Father Morrissey started the STAR job-training program. It was down in the basement of Holy Family school. We had STAR going down there. Then he started Head Start, which has gone on for almost forty years now in Natchez. They have eighteen classes over there now, with twenty students to a class. Father Morrissey didn't get nothing out of it himself, but it created jobs for the people here. He definitely created some jobs because Head Start has something like a $20 million a year budget.

Mary Cecealia Lee

Father Morrissey was a brain, and he was a strong man, very strong. He was a very unique person, and he liked to eat. He could be at a meeting or something, and he'd call up and say, "What do you have in the refrigerator?"

"Father, I have to get up in the morning."

"What do you have in the refrigerator?" And you had to tell him. Then, he'd say, "Well, thaw it out 'cause I'll be over there in so-and-so length of time." He was a funny man. Everybody loved him. He was a go-getter. He didn't just do things with the church and the parishes. He was also a part of the community action agencies here. He was on the board, and they really escalated after he became a part of it, because of that marvelous brain that God gave him. We all learned from him; it's amazing how you can be around a person who's smart and you get smarter from dealing with him.

And he would listen; he was a good listener. Whenever there was a church or community meeting about an issue, we all had our time to say whatever we thought. He was very open-minded. Then, after he'd listen, he would tell you how he felt about it. He was not quick to reply. He would think. You could see him thinking; he would just ponder for a minute. Then he'd say something like, "I think it would be wise if you did this or if you did that." It's not like telling you what to do—just, "I just think it would be wise."

Reverend Shead Baldwin

Father Morrissey worked with us throughout the movement until death claimed him. He was a real fine fellow, one of the finest you'd want to meet. He worked with us through all the negotiations and all of that. The white people hated his guts because he was white, and he would get into it. Every time he would go to say something in our defense, they'd turn red and cut him off. They hated his guts, but Father didn't care. To us in the movement, he was just another one of us. Everybody liked him.

Sidney Gibson

Father Morrissey was probably more involved with the community than the majority of the priests who've been at Holy Family. Father Morrissey was active in civil rights and everything else. He was active in the Community Action Program (CAP), and this kind of thing. We worked together in the CAP program here in the war on poverty. He served as vice president of the organization, and I served as president for about three years.

Father Morrissey was chairman of the Loyal Democrats for a while, and I was voter education coordinator for southwest Mississippi during that time. We worked in all the surrounding counties. We were pretty active in Fayette, around Jefferson County there. In fact, we were participants in the campaign when we got the first black mayor, Charles Evers. Later, Father Morrissey went to work as an advisor to Charles Evers.

Protestant ministers were sort of the dominating force in the civil rights movement, and they, the ministers themselves, wasn't particularly fond of the Catholic Church. I think it might also have been some envy on the part of some of the Protestant ministers, because of the educational qualifications of priests. And they really didn't want people to depend on priests. They figured the people knew Father

Morrissey was well-educated and probably more qualified than others in the community. In fact, he was. I think some ministers started talking about a Catholic takeover of the movement. Father Morrissey and myself was accused of that several times. I heard people say this. But I told them we ought to be able to do what we are obligated to do.

The majority of the people believed in us. They had good reason to believe. Father Morrissey knew a lot of things, and he was respected by just about everybody. He had the ability to develop programs and strategies. He really knew something about organization. In fact, I learned about half of what I know, maybe a little more, from him—just from sitting down and working with him and talking with him and working out different strategies.

We had differences. We didn't agree on everything, but we had respect for each other. We never had a falling out, but we had some strong arguments. When he'd get to the door, he'd say, "I didn't come to socialize today." Then I knew we had something to talk about.

Joe Hall

Father Morrissey was a likable person. He was jolly; he liked to joke around a lot, but he was sincere about seeing justice done and being a part of it. I think it saddened him that more people in the church did not follow his lead. There may even have been some resentment in the church about Father Morrissey putting the place here in a little jeopardy because he was so open in what he did. They worried that somebody might come by and bomb the church, especially when the NAACP office was here. Father Morrissey was elected president of the NAACP chapter in

Natchez. That was pretty unique for a white man who's a Catholic priest.

Father Morrissey was pastor when Vatican II took place, and a lot of changes happened in the church. There is always resistance to change. Some churches resisted these changes; some went right along with everything that was said. The pope said "Do it," so they did it, and Father Morrissey was one of them. We had a big altar in our church, and that was a bone of contention. Father took it down, took the altar rails down, too. I don't think he consulted with anybody. He said we're going to take it down, and that's the way it was done. And man, some people hated that, and I guess almost hated him for doing it. At Cathedral, by the same token, the people of the parish said you're going to take this altar down over our dead bodies, and it's still up. You see, we probably could've had our cake and eaten it, too, just like they did. We could've put an altar down at the front and used the old one as the tabernacle and kept it. But it didn't faze me at the time, because I wasn't into saving historical things. In hindsight, maybe I wish now that it had stayed there for posterity. We could've had the new liturgy facing the people and still kept it. So some of the people that got mad were right in that respect.

Charles Harris and Selma Mackel Harris

Selma: Father Morrissey married us.
Charles: And I remember one thing he said. He asked me, "You sure you want to do this?" Just joking with me, you know, and I said, "Well, I guess so, Father." After he married us, we got a letter from the Mississippi State Department informing us that we hadn't been married. We weren't legally married.

Selma: We'd been married about a year.

Charles: And he didn't ever send in the papers.

Selma: And he called us up and asked us, "Did you get that letter?"

Charles: And he made a joke out of it.

Selma: He was our religion teacher in school.

Charles: And he really made it interesting. He didn't make it humdrum, and he challenged us.

Selma: I'll never forget that's where I learned about slander. Because he was against talking about people, saying things that you weren't sure about, discussing it with other people, and making another person look bad. I'll never forget it. He used to hit that desk and tell us, "I will see to it that none of you will do that." I'll never forget that.

Charles: He made you think; he made you want to do things in your life because he was always encouraging, and he always had a joke. Whatever you didn't do in his class, you had to do after school, so it made you do right in his class. I tell you, he was a real good fellow.

Selma: He sure was. He was strict, in a way, but he was loving. You always knew that he cared about you.

Charles: He pushed, too, and I think he made a few enemies in the white community. That's probably why he ended up in Fayette. I guess he really took his SSJ [Society of St. Joseph] seriously.

Elsie Jackson

I was the secretary of the parish when Father Morrissey came. He was a civil rights man. That was his whole thing. He fought hard for black people's rights. They tried to kill him; they tried to bomb him; they tried to do everything to him. He got many, many, many threats. But Father would just walk up and speak out. He wasn't a person to hide behind anything or anyone.

In Natchez, the black people loved Father Morrissey, and the white folks hated him. Oh, goodness, they hated the ground he walked on. If they could've set him on fire, they would have. They hated him, and they let him know that in no uncertain terms. He'd get three and four [traffic] tickets a day. He'd be going back and forth to Fayette and they'd sit there waiting for him. And there was nothing he could say about it. He paid many a ticket. I've never seen a priest pay as many tickets as he did.

The parish was almost divided over Father Morrissey, too. I guess some people felt that his time wasn't spent on his religious duties. They felt that his concern was nothing about the church or the school; his concern was with civil rights. But, the poor thing, he was trying to work it all together. They didn't understand.

Some people would tell him, "Father, you need to settle down a bit." But he didn't do it. Then the Josephites wanted to take him back to Baltimore, kind of rest him up a bit. He was getting sicker then. He had sugar diabetes, and just kept ripping and running. He wouldn't take his medicine right. And he wouldn't go to Baltimore. So they just gave him a place up in Fayette and told him to stay on up there.

Father Morrissey was a dear person. He was real humble and sweet, but he could raise the devil when he got ready. I loved working with him. He had a good head on his shoulders; he knew his business. He was a beautiful person to work with.

When he finally died, on September 18, 1984, Aubrey Webb buried him from his funeral home. I guess Mr. Laird [owner of the "white" funeral home] wouldn't take him. So Webb buried him. I don't think he really wanted to go any other place. His funeral was held at Holy Family.

Duncan Morgan

Father William Morrissey was probably the most involved white person in the state of Mississippi in the civil rights era. But even Father Morrissey didn't try to force all of the parishioners to become a part of the movement. He worked with individual contacts. But there was no doubt in anybody's mind where the priests of Holy Family stood, and especially him. I guess he was, in some circles, the most loved person in Natchez, and in other circles the most hated. Father Morrissey gave a great bit of the intellectual leadership to the movement. Someone told me, in a discussion one time, that Charles Evers was the mouth of the civil rights struggle in this area; Father Morrissey was the brains.

There was no animosity in the parish about Father Morrissey's role in the movement. Some of us, and I was guilty of this at times, felt that he almost neglected the parish in doing that work. We might have felt that emotionally, but intellectually we knew what he was doing. But everybody in the parish didn't march or anything like that. I personally didn't. I felt that you can lead by example. My thing was to conduct myself in such a way that people, whether they wanted to or not, would have no choice but to respect me. So I didn't have to go with the marches and the things like that. But, oh, there were many other parishioners who were right with him. Nobody was antagonistic toward him for it. And the NAACP office was in the church hall, so that let the community know that the parish was right.

Later the first adult education program, STAR, used the basement of the church building for the offices. So the parish was very much involved. Some of the parishioners enthusiastically supported it; some others went along, but nobody grumbled about it because everybody knew that there was a need, and there was a lot of good being done.

Louisa Quinn

Father Morrissey wouldn't really care what people felt about him, even his parishioners. He was that type of priest. Because, see, some of the blacks didn't attend the civil rights meetings. They were all for them, but they was scared to go. So they felt nothing bad toward Father Morrissey for going to all the meetings.

The police would pick on Father Morrissey. They'd stop and give him tickets and things. He'd say sometimes he was speeding and sometime he wasn't speeding, but they would give him tickets. He was up at Fayette during a lot of this time that he was coming down here to march.

He really was for the blacks, and he showed it in a lot of ways. I remember one night he got out in the street, at the spot where Wharlest Jackson was killed, and prayed, and his conclusion to his prayer was that the only thing he regretted was that he was a white man. And I think that carried a lot of weight with the black people. I believe he meant everything he said, because he didn't have to get out there and march with us or pray with us.

Charles Evers

He was the least known hero of our whole era. I don't know anybody who cared more sincerely about the betterment of mankind than Father Morrissey. He was the only white person at that time to stand up with us, to march with us. They threatened him. They did everything but kill him, and he stayed with us. He was one of my best friends.

(From *The Natchez Democrat*, September 19, 1984)

Chapter 12

Integration

Mary Cecealia Lee

Cathedral had never been integrated; it was considered the white school like St. Mary's was considered the white church. So in 1966, Father William Morrissey spearheaded the integration. He decided that we would do it, and everything was planned. He talked with us and the kids. I think it might've been thirty of us families that were going to participate, but that morning, before school, it had dwindled considerably. People became afraid. My mother wanted to put me out of the house; she was frightened to death. She was also subservient to whites.

It was a very, very difficult time, but I went ahead with it. It was very difficult for my two children who went to the school. I think it was two years before anybody sat to eat with my son Kenny; he had to eat alone for two years. They wouldn't sit at the table, but he refused to leave. He said he would stay there now that he was there, and he stayed. But that's what they did to him. He was hurt, but he wouldn't acknowledge how much.

To this day a lot of the kids he graduated with, if they see me, they'll ask, "How's Kenny?" and that kind of thing. They'll say, "We want to get in touch with him and invite him to our class reunion." But Kenny told me not to give anybody his address. I never tell him about them asking because he doesn't want to hear it. It's just something that is past tense. But he has a good education. He turned out real well. He's an electrical engineer, so he got a good background there.

Kenny went to Cathedral in the sixth grade, and he was the first black to graduate, so it makes me feel good when I see black kids over there now, but Lord, what I would like to say about that place. There was just so much prejudice. They wouldn't let Kenny play on the basketball team, and he loved basketball. The reason they gave for not letting him play was that he was playing at the black school. He would go up to Holy Family and play ball in the afternoons.

I always told him, "If you really don't want to stay, you can leave, but it's important that we do this because there's going to be others come after us, and if we fail, they might never let us back in again."

It wasn't easy for me. As a mother, I wanted to be overly protective I think. I made sure I was there for everything that parents were supposed to be there for. I didn't miss anything. I kept up with his homework and saw that he put time in for study, and his grades were very, very good. I was just there for him all the time. I might have been a bit too protective; and I think that's why he stayed on like he did, because he knew it meant an awful lot to me.

Kenny is still Catholic, but I don't think he's very active because the lady he married is a Lutheran. I sort of think that Cathedral changed that child's mind somewhat about Catholicism. I think he felt like, if these are supposed to be Christians, and they can treat us like this, then I'm not a believer like I was. He was an altar boy all his life, but I think that experience changed his mind. It does do something to you. What makes them think they're so much better than us just because they're white? Did God ever say that we weren't as good as a white person? He never said that. We all die.

I think some of them have come around considerably since that time. My sister's boy, Wesley, went to Cathedral all of his years. He graduated in 1989. I don't think he felt any of the pressure that Kenny did because the way had been paved by then. Things were different. His classmates were in and out of my mother's house; they were staying overnight. During graduation time, they would be having things at their house and inviting Wesley over. He would leave and go places all over with them, so things were much better.

Joe Hall

My children were among the first to go when we integrated Cathedral School. I got seven kids, and I can't remember how many of them were in school at that time. But they were here at Holy Family, and I frankly had no intentions of them going to Cathedral. Then Father Morrissey called me on a weekend and said, "Look, we've gone through all this hell, and now we don't have anybody to go." So I said okay. My oldest daughter was unable to go the first year because they said all the classes were filled. The next year they had a vacancy, and she was able to go. But I'm sure that in itself was just being punitive because in later years I was on the school board up there, and they never turned down any newcomers into town if they were white. I don't care how many they had in class.

But it wasn't all negative. I worked with a man on my job named Bob Drews. He was a white Catholic whose children went to Cathedral, and the first day of the integration, Bob Drews came to me, and he said, "Joe, your children going to school?

I say, "Yeah."

He said, "Don't worry about a thing. We got a group of men; we're going to be there, and it ain't going to be no trouble." You give credit where it's due; he did offer that bit of consolation.

David Lewis

My daughter, Jacqueline, and some more of them was the first ones to integrate Cathedral School. Someone called my wife and told her they were going to have a meeting about Cathedral. There were about four or five families discussing this, and during that fall we registered our kids into Cathedral. We wanted to start someplace, and somebody had to start it. I don't mind taking risks when it benefits my family, and I wanted my kids to have the best education.

After they'd been there for a while, they was accepted. One white girl said how my son, David Tyrone Lewis, was so smart. She said every time the teacher asks a question, he could answer it. And going there helped them a lot because it gave them a sense of being with whites, contact with them, that would help them in the world to come.

But it was a lot of pressure on Jacqueline being one of the first. I didn't know exactly how much it was, but she didn't finish over there. She went to the eleventh grade. Then it was 1970; we went on strike at the plant, and I wasn't able to pay the tuition. The Sister at the school told me to let her come on, but Jackie wanted to be with her friends in the public school. She had a class ring for Cathedral, but she finished in

North Natchez in 1971. When there are two or three blacks in a school and the rest is white, it's a lot of pressure. She never did discuss it with me, but when she saw the opportunity to leave, she was glad to leave. Still, she had some good friends there, too. In fact, one of her friends at school lives in Houston where Jacqueline does now. She's white, and they are very close. When you see one, you'll see the other. They are really close.

Marge Baroni

When the integration of the Catholic schools finally happened in 1966, I had my two youngest children in the public schools, because the Catholic school was so crowded in the lower grades. But when they integrated, I put those two little ones, Mark and David, back over in the Catholic school, because the public schools were still segregated.

When the decision was made to integrate Cathedral School the rule was that only blacks who were Catholics could go there. This was in order not too integrate it too fully and not to make it too open—not to do the job thoroughly. Still there was an exodus of whites. This was in 1966. So white Catholic children went to the still segregated public schools, and then the next year the public schools were integrated. Then these private academies began to go up around here, the so-called Christian academies. So those Catholic children, whose parents didn't want them mingling with blacks, would go to the Christian academies. That was their last resort.

Meanwhile, some of the Episcopalians, Methodists, and others didn't want to send their children to the inferior academies. The first ones were started by people who had been in the Klan, and they were looked down on by the aristocrats. So some of the higher-class types wouldn't send their children to what they considered low-class Christian academies, so they sent them to our nice Catholic school, Cathedral. They felt that a little bit of integration was better than a whole lot in the public schools.

It was such a dreadful time for the children, because there had been no preparation by the administration of the school. They were afraid to sit down and give the children a course in human relations. Some of the Sisters did, but they were on their own.

Herman Mazique

I went to school at Cathedral around 1966, the year that they changed over. I was in the eighth grade. My mother [Mamie Mazique] was such a strong advocate for civil rights back in that time. She only wanted what was best. That's why she stuck me in Cathedral. She didn't know I was going to be abused and have to go through all this type of stuff. We had to make a change. Somebody had to try to integrate the school. Somebody had to go over there first and suffer the abuse.

They were very prejudiced. The white students would kick my desk around. I mean, they didn't want me sitting by them. They would spit on us, paint stuff on our lockers, and put stuff in our lockers. We would walk through the hallway; they'd trip us. They thought maybe we was the first two or three blacks to go over there, and they was going to get rid of that. Representative Johnny Junkins, an elected official here in Natchez, used to sit behind me, and he would kick my chair all the way up to the front almost. I would take it, bring my chair back. Nobody in the classroom would say anything, even the instructor. Johnny Junkins will pass by me today on the street and still won't speak, after twenty-some years of knowing me. I'm serious. One of the men who used to hit me in the head while I was playing basketball, his name was Geohagen, and he would not speak to me either, until he came back from Vietnam. He had both his legs cut off, and I guess he got over there and found out that blood was blood.

I had to try to get the white students to help me to learn. I didn't know that Cathedral was so advanced. We were so uneducated, and some of us could not even stay there. I went to Cathedral for a year, and it was just so abusive. I couldn't get tutoring; I couldn't get help. I was having such a hard time. I would take tests and fail. I mean, it would hurt my feelings. Marge Baroni tried to get her daughters to speak or say something, but they were scared to death, and you couldn't blame them.

I couldn't take it, and I left. I went to public school. I had never drank a beer in my life, never drank a bottle of wine. I got over there to public school; the next thing you know, I'm smoking cigarettes in the bathroom. I'm drinking wine in the auditorium. I'm skipping class, something we never did. Your parents, still, were tough on you, but, I'm telling you, we just ran into a different standard at school. Most of us went on and completed high school, but when we first got there, we went plumb, buck wild. We still attended church, but, eventually, that started to sink away for some people.

Mamie Mazique

Herman went to Holy Family. When they started trying to desegregate Cathedral, I didn't want to move him over there, but finally we did because Kenneth Lee, Mary Cecealia Lee's son, was over there by himself. We asked Herman if he would go over there with Kenneth, and he said, "Yeah." That was one of my downfalls. It was a mistake I made for him. I sent him over there trying to help, and, then, when he got over there, they mistreated him. They isolated him, and he had a hard time over there. It caused his grades to fall, and he had a problem getting books, and it just wasn't good for him over there. They harassed us here at home about him being there, and it was just bad. They harassed him on the phone and at school.

Herman wouldn't tell me about it. But finally, Marge Baroni's daughter, Roseanne, really got worried about him and started telling Ms. Baroni about what was happening. Ms. Baroni started telling me, and I went up and talked to the teachers about it several times. Finally, people started calling me, telling me that if I didn't get him out of there, they was going to kill him. I was going to find him out by the old barbecue pit out there.

So we finally decided that it was best to move him, and we did. But he couldn't go back to Holy Family, so we had to move him to the public school, and that wasn't good. By then he had really gotten confused, and he just didn't know what was happening. He had been brought up sort of sheltered here at home and at Holy Family.

It just didn't end up in his best interest. We were trying to help the school and the community, and that's the result of it. I'm not bitter about it, but I wish it hadn't happened because if this hadn't happened, maybe Herman could've kept his bearings and ended up a normal person because, up until that time, I never had any problem out of him. Then, after he left Holy Family and went to Cathedral, and then to public school, that's when I started having problems.

Herman did finally graduate from public high school, and he got a four-year scholarship to Jackson State. But by then he was kind of messed up. He was kind of confused. I don't know if he had begun to mess with anything like pills or cough syrup, or anything like that, but he went on into Jackson State, and the first year he did well. He had a high average, and the second year he did well, but he began to move about. Then, we had to kind of clamp down on him and try to check him, you know. He had started to skip classes, and he moved out of one dorm to another, and then he wanted to move into an apartment, and I'm sure he was into drugs and drinking, and his grades began to fall.

I don't fault the children at Cathedral for what happened to Herman. I fault the parents. But, you know, they helped to destroy my child. I was trying to help others, and I paid a big cost.

Wilbur Johnson

The civil rights movement made it possible for Natchez to get blacks involved in all aspects of everything. Politically, we have aldermen, we have black aldermen; we have black supervisors; we have blacks on almost every board that's functioning in the area; we got blacks in the banks. Almost every business that hopes to succeed is going to have to have a black employed in it; we got blacks at all the schools except the private schools that've been set up for the particular purpose of not having any. There is communication between the races.

But education-wise I think that it has been a setback. I think the integration process was very beneficial, but I think integration has really hurt blacks as far as education is concerned. I guess we were under the impression that, if we were able to intermingle with whites, our educational level would jump tenfold. But somehow our young people have picked the wrong values, and we are going in the opposite direction. We've gotten away from the neighborhood concept and living together as a community. And I attribute part of it to the integration process.

Chapter 13

Black and Catholic Today

Louisa Quinn

Since the civil rights movement, there's been a lot more going back and forth with the Cathedral parish. The Cathedral priests come to our church, and we go there. We all eat together now. They have programs, or dinners, and we're invited. We invite Cathedral around to Holy Family, too. For instance, this year, we'll host the graduates from Cathedral High School, and the next year, Cathedral will do it. We even had a funeral for one of our parishioners held at Cathedral this year, so you know we've come a long ways.

Eugene Dottery

I hope Holy Family will continue as it has been, and I also hope the school can continue because that is the life of Holy Family. At one time, they even mentioned the idea of just dropping the church and having everybody go to Cathedral. It was just a thought; it never was discussed too much, but I'd hate to see something like that. Things are a lot better now, but I believe it will take another hundred years for white and black people to get along like they should. It'll take that long to get some of that hatred, that fear, out of the people.

Elsie Jackson

Today Holy Family School just goes through grade six, but I hope it will continue as an elementary school. At least the kids can get a foundation. You don't put down public school, because everyone can't pay to get an education, but our children need this. They need the religion; they need the caring; they need the love, and Holy Family is the only place they're going to get it. If this is gone, you can forget it. You can even forget about the church if the school goes. There won't be any interest then.

And I think our Catholic Church has something great to offer the African American community, if they'll come and accept it. We are Christians on this hill. Other people should come and find out what we are all about. Our church has been a learning center for our black people. The whole bit— not just coming to church, kneeling, and standing—but it teaches you about the world and what black people have to face. This is what it has done for me. You have some black people that really don't understand the world, the people in it, or anything, and they don't know anything about Christ. You've got to learn to respect yourself first, and then you'll get all the respect in the world from someone else, and this is what we need because we have a lot of black people with no self-esteem, no respect, no nothing out there.

Ora Frazier

I look at Holy Family School today as a place of hope for children who are searching and whose families are searching for something that's better than what they could get in a larger setting. We are small. Our average is like twenty children to a classroom, and Holy Family School has just been a place where parents would feel comfortable for the children to be, at the same time, knowing that they're going to get a strong academic program.

I spoke with the education director at the diocese in Jackson week before last, and he was very pleased with what we're doing here. He said, "You've got to stay open," and that was the one thing I wanted to hear him say. But he also said, "You're going to have to go up on your tuition. You cannot keep quality people if you don't pay them." We have two retired teachers with master's degrees who made a record for themselves in the public school, so they're getting their retirement checks plus what we give them. We have one lady who has her master's, who's been at Holy Family twenty-two years, and she tells me constantly, "I could've been gone a long time, but I like it here. I don't have the problems that I know I would have in the public school." And, she said, "We're just such a family here."

Ajani Thomas

I went to this school because my father went here all twelve years, and then he went to college at another school. My grandfather came to this school also, and he had some friends here like the Sisters and a priest. Some of the children used to be dissin' one of our priests and he'd always say, "Don't be messing with Father." He thinks this is a better place than the public schools, where there are more bullies and people acting nasty and bad things, not the kind of stuff you need to know to grow up.

I like science and math, except for subtraction, of course, and reading and social studies, but especially science.

I think the best part of school is when we have recess and stop all our hard work and academics and stuff like that, and we get to have some free time and play.

We also learn that God is the Creator of all things. We were studying the Creation this week, how God stepped out into space until he said, "That's good," when he had the earth hurled up below him. And how he toiled at the mud just to make Adam in his own form and blew the breath of life into him, and then he made all the animals and the birds and the fish and the beasts and the fowl and all those creatures. And we learned that he sent his only son, and his only son sacrificed his life just so we could be able to go back to heaven and enjoy the bountifuls of heaven.

When we have Mass at school, I like the singing. I like "Immaculate Mary," "Hail, Holy Queen," and the "Gloria." I also like listening to the sermon, what the Bible really was about, and sometimes I try to picture the sermon or the Bible reading in my mind, and I'm successful sometimes.

Sylvester Matthews

Some of my friends in my neighborhood ask me why I keep coming to Holy Family School, and I tell them because this is the only school where I can find plenty of friends and I can find out about my African heritage and where I came from. A Catholic education teaches you not to exclude anybody just for the color of their skin or their religion or what they're wearing, to include everybody, even if they're not as perfect as you are.

If I could talk to schoolchildren someday, I'd like to tell everyone how important it is to read books because books can help you find out lots of things. I would tell them how important it is to get an education because we used to not have the opportunity to get an education.

One of the things I like most about Holy Family School is that you're always able to take holy communion. Some people aren't able to take holy communion yet, but it feels good to have that privilege. My favorite song at Mass is "One Bread and One Body."

Wilbur Johnson

I have tremendous hope for Holy Family. I'm on the school board, so I'm going to talk about the school first, then I'm going to talk about the church. We are trying to move Holy Family to one of the top elementary schools in this area for K through six. We're going to try to get the best qualified personnel and offer better opportunities. We got a new concert band, for instance. And we just hope that we're going to be able to grow. Our biggest problem is money. However, we're just going to try to find some way, the Lord bless us, through the projects and proposals and grant-writing to get something. We feel as though the Lord will help us in some kind of way.

As far as the church is concerned, we have several drives. Physically, we need an elevator; we need some repairs. Holy Family's at a point where we got to do a lot of work on it, but I see a great future for Holy Family.

As far as church is concerned, we're experiencing something now that a lot of people are not ready for or don't understand. We are being permitted to participate in the Mass according to our culture—black culture—instead of the idea that someone has given us of another man's culture. Some of our parishioners are not ready for it. They feel as though it is sacrilegious to stomp your feet and say "Amen" or "Thank you, Lord." They like the old traditional way of kneeling down and being quiet. Even though your heart is bursting to say "Amen," hold it in. So we got a struggle there, but, eventually they'll look and see others and become more aware and let themselves go and say "Amen," too.

This style of Mass is new for me, too, but I like it. I'm like some of the old ones; it takes me a little bit. I'm not the one that says "Amen," but I find myself beginning to mumble a little bit, and beginning to clap my hands, and I don't mind raising my hands, and I don't mind saying "Thank you, Lord," and it feels good.

Lavera Gibson Allen

With all the changes over the years, it's still Holy Family. I guess it's like baking a cake: if you find a good recipe, you don't want to change it. I know the changing of the nuns' habits and the priests' collars has done some good. It's got to be a whole lot more comfortable, and it brings the nuns and priests closer to the people. But I still miss the '60s. If you don't have a past to bring you forward, then you don't have a future to go to.

David Lewis

A lot of our parishioners don't realize it's a changing world, and some of them still don't go anyplace, don't visit other churches. I have been to churches where they have girls serving on the altar, and here they look around like there's something wrong with it. Now they've gotten around to the full gospel choir. It's a big part of our African American heritage, and most of them like the choir. But we still have some who don't. When I go to church in Houston, they have a choir, a flute, and a drum. They have a wonderful time over there.

Barbara Washington

Our kids need Holy Family. This is the only school that they have to identify themselves with, the black kids. The doors are open for anybody, but we need Holy Family. We need it bad, even though it doesn't go any further than the sixth grade now. The children get this religion background and they get their "blackground."

Charles Harris and Selma Mackel Harris

Selma: My thing with Holy Family is that there's not enough support for the school, and I think we in the black community need a school in order for our kids to know their black heritage. We have to find financial means to continue the school.

Charles: I would echo that. We need this school today basically because of our heritage. We're not getting it anyplace else. My wife and I were taught by white nuns and priests, so we didn't learn anything about our heritage, but in our time there was a black public school, and a lot of our friends went to that school, so we came in contact with them and learned a lot about our heritage, but today they don't. Holy Family Catholic Church needs to survive because today it's actually a beacon in the community. All of the churches in this area, I feel, look up to us. I think we are actually the only church in the community that you can look at that's been the same since it started. I think they look up to us that way because, believe it or not, in recent years we've had a lot of people joining our church from the Protestant churches. There's evidently something that they see. And the school is very important; I tell my wife all the time, if we're going to have a school to support, we need to be the best school in the community. Every kid that leaves here should be academically ready for whatever school they go to. We're going to get the religion, no doubt about it; that's a must. And it may be that this school could actually help turn the black community around in this town, because the kids will return to being taught by black men and women about themselves, about their history, and what they can be and what they cannot be.

We've lost a lot of that. In the desegregated public schools our kids have mostly white teachers. And it's very important that we get it again because that's what actually made the black race move forward in the past. I'm not a segregationist, but I do believe that, for us to regain our self-respect and esteem, it's going to have to come from us, and it's going to have to come from our black men and women and teachers. It's very important. Until we reach the maturity to realize that we can function in the society, the only way we're going to get there is through our people. We're going to have to go back to that. We fought so hard for integration, but we wanted integration in the sense of, "I want the same job; I want to be able to go the same place." We didn't want integration to take away all our teachers.

So, Holy Family Church and School can be a viable part of the community. We're going to have to promote this school to make it survive. We're going to have to promote blackness and our black culture and make the people in the community understand that the way we're going to survive is through that self-esteem. When black people walk out of that school, even in the sixth grade, when they go anywhere, they're ready; they know about themselves as a people, and they are ready academically. That's my last sermon.

Lucille Royal Mackel

I think Holy Family Catholic Church has meant a lot to Natchez. It has been struggling for a long, long time, and it's still there, you know. We have the "Southern Road to Freedom" program now, explaining all the life of the black people that were known here in Natchez. I went to one of the programs one Thursday night, and the whites that were there—tourists from out of town—they really and truly appreciated finding out about black heritage. They got involved in the singing. They went up there and sang with the people and just had a good time. It was very enlightening.

Chapter 14

A Southern Road to Freedom

It's eight o'clock on a Thursday night in March 2002, and the pews of First Presbyterian Church in downtown Natchez are filled to overflowing. It's not a church crowd. People are casually dressed and talking loudly, but the demographics seem about right for First Presbyterian. The people are mostly white-skinned, gray-haired, and prosperous, but it's not a Natchez crowd. The voices are mostly from up North. A podium sits in the middle of the stage at the front of the church, with a set of risers on each side.

At about five after eight, a stylishly dressed black man sits down at an electronic piano. He begins to play gospel-style. In about five minutes people begin to walk out of back doors behind the stage and file onto the risers. They are nineteen men and women. Their ages appear to range from late teens to early seventies. All are wearing African robes and headdresses made from colorful fabric printed in bold patterns. They stand in silence, looking out at the audience with solemn, determined expressions. The pianist continues to play.

At the podium a narrator begins to read the story of slavery in Natchez. He tells about the slave market at the Forks of the Road and the cruel abuse of a people stolen from homes and torn away from families. The people on the risers begin to sing, "Walk with Me Lord." As the choir sings, several black people,

158

dressed in black, walk down the center aisle of the church. They have shackles on their ankles and wrists and iron collars around their necks. They are chained one to another. They walk slowly, with their heads down. When they reach the front of the church they stand before the stage, facing the audience, heads still down-turned, while the choir sings, "Go Down Moses."

This is the opening scene of "Southern Road to Freedom," a chorale presentation put on three times a week during the Natchez Pilgrimage by the Holy Family Catholic Church Choir. For decades, Natchez African Americans watched millions of white visitors pass through their town. The tourists came from all over the United States and from all over the world, and they left knowing less about the Deep South than they did when they arrived. In the early decades of Pilgrimage, they saw the myth of an Old South aristocracy set against stereotypes of grinning, singing and dancing, watermelon-eating black people. Then they saw the airbrushed falsification that is presented today. Finally, lay leaders at Holy Family Catholic Church stepped into the breech and began producing their own program to give Pilgrimage visitors the rest of the story.

"Southern Road to Freedom" draws full houses every year. The Natchez Pilgrimage experience gives visitors the chance to sample Southern cuisine and culture, to savor the undeniable aesthetic charm of the old mansions, and maybe to hit the jackpot at the casino under the hill. And now, with the presentation of "Southern Road to Freedom," it is even possible for the visitor to experience two hours of undiluted truth served up with the fervor and swing of the African American gospel tradition.

At the podium the narrator goes on to tell the story of Ibrahima, a prince from Timbuktu, in what is now Mali, who was enslaved and ended up in Natchez. Decades later an English visitor recognized the prince as the son of a man who had saved his life in Timbuktu. The Englishman pleaded with Ibrahima's owner to free him. He offered to buy the prince's freedom. But the owner refused to part with his most valuable slave. Ibrahima grew old in slavery. Finally he was freed when his owner died, and friends bought him a ticket back to Africa. He landed on the western coast, but died before reaching his inland home.

"Go down, Moses," sings the choir. *"Let my people go."*

Next come stories of runaways, and slave resistance, and a visit to Mississippi by the fabled "Black Moses," Harriet Tubman, who led hundreds of slaves north to freedom.

"Steal away..." the music calls, *"steal away to Jesus. Steal away, steal away home. I ain't got long to stay here."*

The runaways had to keep running all the way to Canada, but some slaves gained their freedom in Natchez and made their own way in the antebellum South. One was Robert Smith, who owned a taxi business and was a sexton of this very First Presbyterian Church. Another was William Johnson, the barber of Natchez, a free person of color and himself a slave owner. Johnson kept a diary that was later published and hailed as the best written document of daily life in a nineteenth-century Southern town.

"I am blessed. Oh, Lord, I am blessed. For all the worst and all the best, I am blessed."

Then came Emancipation and Reconstruction and new opportunities for the children of Africa. August and Sarah Mazique saved their money and became landowners. Eventually their chain of plantations even included "Oakland," the estate upon which they had worked as slaves. Some Mazique descendants became members of Holy Family Catholic Church and one of them, Mamie, served as secretary of the Natchez NAACP during the civil rights movement of the 1960s.

"Precious Lord, take my hand. Lead me on, help me stand."

J. R. Lynch had been a house slave at Dunleith, a famous mansion that is on the Pilgrimage tour and is operated year-round as a bed-and-breakfast. During Reconstruction, he became speaker of the Mississippi House of Representatives and was elected to the U.S. Congress. Lynch also wrote and published three books about his experiences in public life. Robert Wood, an African American Catholic and former slave, was elected mayor of Natchez in 1871.

"I'm going to lay down my sword and shield, down by the riverside....I ain't gonna study war no more."

Alice Sims and Jane Johnson were slaves at the Melrose estate before the war. When the property was abandoned, they stayed on. They maintained the grounds and protected the mansion and its furnishings for twenty years. They lived at Melrose into the 1930s and 1940s, respectively, and helped its twentieth-century owner restore it. The grand house and grounds these two African American women struggled to save were later purchased by the National Park Service and are open to visitors year-round. Now it is the only antebellum mansion tour in Natchez at which you not only hear about the slaves, but see how they actually lived and labored.

"Oh, freedom. Oh, freedom. Oh, freedom over me. Before I'll be a slave, I'll be buried in my grave and go home to my Lord to be free."

The song and the story continue. After an intermission, the singers return wearing traditional choir robes, and the narration picks up with the founding of the city's historic African American churches—Rose Hill Baptist, Zion Chapel AME, and Holy Family Catholic. The first pastor of Zion AME, Hiram Revels, also became a U.S. Senator in 1870, and then came home to serve as president of Alcorn College, now Alcorn State University.

After the choir sings a song called, "Highway to Heaven," something strange happens. Robed choir members come down from the risers and walk out into the crowd. There they walk up to members of the audience, take them by the hands, and lead them up to the stage. Soon the choir is crowded off the risers, and the entire stage is filled with an assembly made up equally of black people in choir robes and white people in casual street clothes. Then they all begin to sing, "This little light of mine, I'm gonna let it shine...." The rest of the crowd joins in. The invisible walls are broken. Reconciliation is established, and freedom is real—right here, right now.

"Amazing grace, how sweet the sound, that saved a wretch like me. I once was lost, but now I'm found. I was blind, but now I see...."

The program continues a little longer, with tributes to artistic greats of black Natchez—singer Elizabeth Greenfield, who performed for Queen Victoria, jazz pianist Bud Scott, and Richard Wright whose novel *Native Son* transformed

American literary culture. There is also a remembrance of the Rhythm Nightclub fire, which killed two hundred young black people. This portion of the program also brings the only secular song on the choir's playlist, George Gershwin's "Summertime."

Finally, sometime after 10:00 p.m., the program concludes. The crowd stands and cheers. The choir bows. But everyone is tired. At last, the crowd slowly makes its way up the aisles. Some stop to buy tapes of the performance or African crafts from a table in the back. The rest make their way to their out-of-state cars, tour buses, and RVs. Their ears are ringing with music. Their heads are jumbled with names and dates they'll never remember. But that isn't the point anymore. Maybe they came to be fair, to hear the other side of the story, and because they heard the music was good. And they got all of that, but they may have gotten something more. You could call it an offering, or a gift. It came in that moment when the Holy Family Choir walked into the crowd and pulled people up to join them. The gesture seemed to say, "This story of suffering is our story, but now it's your story too....This music, this culture, this faith—it's all ours. We brought it from Africa and hid it for years. We passed it from parent to child. It's ours. But come on up; it belongs to all of us, now."

It was an offering of redemption and reconciliation. It's an offering that could redeem a nation and a state. It could even redeem a city by a river, on a hill, sitting at the forks of the road.

"...'Twas grace that taught my heart to fear, and grace my fear relieved. How precious did that grace appear, the hour I first believed...."

Source Notes

From January to June 1994, Reverend Tim Murphy, Glenmary, made several trips to Natchez, Mississippi, to interview 44 members and associates of Holy Family Catholic Church and students at Holy Family School. Tapes of these interviews are stored at the Glenmary Research Center in Nashville, Tennessee, as are transcripts of the interviews in hard copy and digital formats. Following is a list of all the people interviewed for this project.

ADAMS, LILLIAN JOHNSON *(Holy Family parishioner, former cook for the school Sisters, later public librarian)*

ALLEN, LAVERA GIBSON

BALDWIN, SHEAD *(Baptist minister and former president of the Natchez NAACP)*

BARONI, LOUIS

BATIESTE, RAYFORD

DAVIS, JULIA

DENNIS, MARIE BYRD

DOTTERY, EUGENE

FLEMING, HARRY

FLEMING, WILLIE *(Converted to Catholicism while a student at St. Francis School; resident of the rural community of Cranfield, Mississippi, outside Natchez)*

FRAZIER, JOE *(Holy Family parishioner and public school principal)*

FRAZIER, ORA (with Joe) *(Holy Family parishioner and principal of Holy Family School)*

GIBSON, SIDNEY *(Paper-mill worker, union leader, and civil rights activist)*

HALL, JOE

HARRIS, CHARLES, JR. (with Selma)

HARRIS, SELMA MACKEL (with Charles Jr.)

HARRIS, CHARLES, SR.

HOGGATT, LAURA (with Adams, Lillian Johnson)

HOGGATT, MARGIE

JACKSON, EDITH

JACKSON, ELSIE *(Lifelong member of Holy Family Church)*

JOHNSON, WILBUR

LARRY, JACOB

LEE, MARY CECEALIA

LEWIS, DAVID

LEWIS, LETTIE

Mackel, Lucille Royal

Marshall, Hattie Rose

Matthews, Sylvester *(Holy Family fifth-grade student)*

Mazique, Herman

Mazique, Mamie *(Holy Family alumnus; Natchez NAACP secretary)*

Montgomery, David

Morgan, Duncan

Parker, Willie Dorsey

Plummer, Robert

Posey, Charles

Quinn, George (with Louisa)

Quinn, Louisa *(Holy Family parishioner jailed during the civil rights movement)*

Rolax, Mazie Belle

Thomas, Ajani *(Holy Family fourth-grade student)*

Washington, Barbara

Washington, Selma Mackel

Webb, Aubrey

Williams, Vernon *(Member of Holy Family Parish Council)*

In addition, there are three tapes of interviews with Holy Family School students from kindergarten through grades six, recorded on May 19, 1994.

Josephite archivist, Reverend Peter Hogan, SSJ, supplied clippings and interview transcripts relevant to the history of Holy Family in Natchez. The quotations from Marge Baroni that appear in this book are from the transcript of Hogan's interview with Mrs. Baroni and Reverend William Morrissey, SSJ. The quotation from Charles Evers, at the end of chapter 11, is from a clipping in the Josephite files.

In addition, Professor Richard Tristano, of St. Mary's University of Minnesota, on behalf of the Glenmary Research Center, conducted considerable archival research into the original establishment of Holy Family as a separate African American parish in Natchez. In 1998, some of that material, and his conclusions, were published as "Holy Family Parish: The Genesis of an African-American Catholic Community in Natchez, Mississippi" in volume 83, number 4 of *The Journal of Negro History* (p. 258).

For information on access to the oral history transcripts, tapes, and other materials, contact: Glenmary Research Center, 1312 Fifth Avenue North, Nashville, TN 37208. Phone: 615-256-1905, Fax: 615-251-1472, or Email: *grc@glenmary.org*

Index